WHEN PENGUINS ATTACK!

BY TOM TOMORROW

ST. MARTIN'S GRIFFIN ❦ NEW YORK

Also by Tom Tomorrow

Greetings from This Modern World
Tune in Tomorrow
The Wrath of Sparky
Penguin Soup for the Soul

E-mail Tom Tomorrow at tomorrow@well.com, or visit the Tom Tomorrow web site (www.thismodernworld.com), where you'll find animations, rarities, and more information about Tom than any sane person would ever want to read, as well as some T-shirts and hats and other consumer products available for your *shopping enjoyment!* Tom is also available for campus speaking engagements, at which he will enlighten, inform, entertain and bedazzle with his multimedia *cartoon extravaganza!* Well, actually, he mostly just shows slides and talks about stuff, but it's fun, really.

www.stmartins.com

The following cartoons originally appeared in a slightly different format in the publications indicated:

pp. 23–25—cover of *The Village Voice* (9/23/99); p. 51—*TV Guide* (9/4/99); pp. 70–71—*The New Yorker* (9/27/99); pp. 88–89—*The Village Voice* (10/12/99); p. 97—*New York Times* Op-Ed page (1/11/00); p. 109—*New York Times* Op-Ed page (3/10/00); pp. 117–119—*The New Yorker* (11/22/99)

ISBN 0-312-20974-6

First Edition: September 2000

10   9   8   7   6   5   4   3   2   1

INTRODUCTION

by Dave Eggers

My first question is an important one: Is Tom Tomorrow—but first we have to get rid of the pseudonym, because we are being serious here, and he's not fooling anyone anyhow, so let's ask the question in the most straightforward possible way, that way being: Is Dan Perkins the best political cartoonist in America?

(Very brief pause, followed by a small chuckle betraying the humor in the question.)

Well of course he is.

Now sure, the field is a dismal one. The medium is moribund and for the most part exasperatingly slow to move past the one-panel, bad-metaphored, brutally obvious and clumsy way these cartoons have been done for centuries. And so being atop such a heap is fine, but not as impressive as being atop, say, the National League home run slugging list. (How about that Mark McGwire!)

There are other cartoonists who are close. A dozen maybe. Or maybe four or five. Actually, there is one more who is close, and his name is Ted Rall. There is also Reuben Bolling, but he is only occasionally political, so is disqualified. But together these three do represent truly the only hope for the genre, because they are the only ones whose work has much at all to do with how we think now—(how can the average mid-season replacement comedy be so much more savvy, more sophisticated than the vast majority of political cartoons, products of this should-be sophisticated medium?) —and how visual communications have evolved in the last twenty years. For instance, are we still fans of cartoons where everything is labeled to indicate the meaning behind each visual metaphor—where the giant shoe descending from the sky is labeled "TARIFFS" and those underfoot are "BUSINESSPEOPLE" and "WORKERS" and such? Are we still fans of this sort of thing, and also, more importantly, are we fans of crosshatching? I would posit that perhaps we are not. Fans of either. Especially crosshatching.

Nor are we fans of the cartoon where the man or couple or family is watching TV, from which some appalling message is emanating, and the man says something indicating his exasperation, something like "What's next, guns in kindergartens?!"

Sure it's hilarious, but still.

Every year we have for our usage more and more varied and sophisticated media and technology, and in every artistic medium practitioners break new ground and react against their predecessors, pushing the form further, or back, then further again, left and right, restless, as artists are born to be, unless they become rich. But restless? Are these artists? These cartoonists? Are they?

No.

So. Dan is atop this stinky heap. But why? What makes him good, and why do so many papers run his work and readers depend upon him?

Yes there's the pure, molten sex appeal. Dan's exploits have been gossiped about for years, and his prowess documented in any number of cartoonist-porn magazines. And while this is surely a key to his popularity, could this account for *all* of his success? Does endurance like his win Pulitzers, which (I think) Dan has won three of?

I say nay. I say nay and when I do I rhyme. Say and nay rhyme. Hi.

Here are some reasons why Dan is the best:

1) His work is didactic, which is what political cartoons should be.

2) His work is virtually the only graphically innovative stuff being produced in the genre.

3) His cartoons pack, in their four word-choked panels, ten times the information and, more importantly, funny laffs, than the average cartoon, even if that cartoon features the clever device where the artist will draw himself under the main panel, he at his drafting table, making one last, pithy and devastating parting comment on a given issue.

4) His cartoons occasionally contain cursing, and frequently contain aliens from outer space. Both are essential to good cartooning.

Am I off-track? Do I meander? Do I end too many questions with question marks? Now, while off-track and meandering, I would like to hike into the woods for a second—come, follow me; those shoes will do fine—and tell you about Dan and his wife, whose name is Beverly. (Sorry ladies, he's taken.) Okay, for many years now I have known Dan. We first met shortly after I moved to the Bay Area, and just weeks after I had started doing my own weekly political cartoon, which was running in the precise spot in the *San Francisco Weekly* that *This Modern World* had run just a month before, before Dan sold out and moved to the *Bay Guardian,* which is owned by Sony and edited in Malaysia. So. After a while, because Dan was stealing my ideas (like, the whole notion of combining words and pictures to comment on current events) and I was nice enough to let him, Dan and I became pals, eventually fought over a handful of women—they were very small women, no more than five inches tall—did Mardi Gras and Bangkok in a crazy, crazy way, and made it through without too many scars, if you know what I mean, ha ha.

Yes. You know, the thing about Dan is this: He is every bit the cranky bastard that he comes off as. For instance, you often meet actors or writers whose real-life personalities do not at all match with their on-screen or on-paper personas. You know who would have surprised you? Flip Wilson. Sure he seemed, on screen, very charming, and droll, and with a certain joie de vivre. Great clothes. But you'd meet the guy and the first thing he'd want to do is punch you. Like: Hi Flip. Punch. Hey Flip. Punch. That's how it went with him. One then the other. Greeting, then a punch. And he always wore very small nylon jogging shorts, much like Mr. Dole and Mr. Gore are apt to, because they each have such nice thighs. Mr. Wilson also had nice thighs, but still.

Well, you'll never see Dan in too-tight jogging shorts. Nor will you be surprised when you sit down for a beer with Dan, which you will never do because he hates his fans and thinks those who buy his books losers. The point is, he is as he seems. In his work, Dan comes off like he's mad about things, that he cares passionately about universal health care and gun control and inequity and hypocrisy, and then you meet him, and guess what? He does indeed does care about all of those things. Except hypocrisy, which he secretly loves.

Now, about Bev. Yes, Dan and Bev are first cousins. And their union is illicit and they asked me not to reveal this to you, the reader (loser) at home. The thing is, Dan was, for the five or so years I first knew him, a very cranky asshole-type bastard. He was cranky in person, and cranky in his cartoon, and often punched me, even when he knew I still bore bruises from the Mr. Wilson mentioned above. But then something happened. He first told me about Beverly while we were eating at a Chinese restaurant on Geary Boulevard, deep in the avenues of San Francisco. We had taken off our shoes, and he talked about having met this woman at a reading or conference somewhere, New Haven maybe, and when he talked about her, all the energy he usually spent dismantling HMOs or the NRA or whatever other evil acronym had recently crawled up his rectum, he was using in a new and different way. He said the word "astonishing" about twelve or thirteen times. He gestured a lot. He was thinking about moving from San Francisco to New Haven to be with this woman. He had lost his mind. He was in love.

And move to New Haven he did, for a year, this high-flying, womanizing cartoonist moved to New Haven to live with a woman who was not yet his wife though had a wife-like name and was his first cousin. Now they are married and, as I write this, they are about to move to a new home, which happens to be exactly two blocks away from my own current home in Brooklyn, New York. This development, naturally, scares me.

What scares me is this: Dan will come over to my house. He will walk into my brother's room, where there hangs a huge painting Dan made and gave to us when he first left San Francisco. It is a giant version of one of those "Greetings from . . ." postcards from the fifties, and within the large block letters of SAN FRANCISCO, he has imbedded and colored many of his usual cast of timely yet timeless characters—Biff, Joan, Marge, the rest of the gang culled from that single, 1954 issue of *LIFE.* The painting is big and gorgeous, and has hung in our homes for many years, in Berkeley and San Francisco, Manhattan and now Brooklyn. Does it look like something you'd expect Angry Man Dan to do? Not at all. Its gleeful colors and cheery imagery—without any sarcasm, please note—betray the fact that Dan is only superficially grumpy, and that just below that grumpiness is the kind of man who paints absurdly happy pictures of our beloved San Francisco, who overflows with hope for the Left after the WTO protests, who still gets apoplectic when he hears Rush Limbaugh or Newt Gingrich or Strom Thurmond, and also the kind of man who still uses the word "astonishing" every time he mentions his wife's name.

My point is you have to love and care about everything and anyone before you can be upset about anything at all. And so the crankiest asshole-bastards, including the filthy man who sits on my steps at night, yelling at passersby about betrayal and Armageddon, well, that stinky dirt-encrusted man is probably the most loving man the world has yet known. Or at least he might be. Wouldn't that make a good story?

I have again lost my way. Back to the issue at hand: The reason I am scared about Dan moving nearby is that it seems inevitable that he will now visit more often and eventually he will want to take, from my poor brother, the "Greetings from San Francisco" painting, because artists always, eventually, want to be reunited with all the work they've sold or given away. And when he comes to get it, we will fight. And he will pull a gun, which he always seems to be doing. And we will struggle with the gun, and it will go off. Neither of us will be harmed, but the hole in the wall will be large, and it will be too late in the evening to purchase spackling compound, and we will be stuck until morning, Dan and I, two characters in a drama called *Life,* written by Sam Shepard and starring Philip Seymour Hoffman and John C. Reilly, in alternating roles.

These are the best cartoons money can buy. It is now summer in Brooklyn. Rage is so close to love—they wear their hair in a very similar way—that people sometimes get them confused. Please read this with soft hands and squinty eyes.

Dave Eggers
May 2000

PREFACE

by Tom Tomorrow

This is my fifth book collection, and since each of these books contains about two years' worth of cartoons, that means that this one could be said to mark my tenth anniversary as a cartoonist. This would, of course, be a completely misleading and inaccurate statement, since I have been drawing cartoons of one sort or another since about the age of five, and since *This Modern World* actually first began to appear in print around 1987 or so. But those first few years involved a lot of experimentation, a lot of thrashing around trying to figure out exactly what it was I wanted to do, and much of the work produced during that period bears as much relation to the cartoon as it exists today as our slack-jawed cave-dwelling ancestors bear to George W. Bush—maybe a little less, now that I think about it—so, let's just call it an even ten years and break out the good china, okay?

Ten years. How in god's name did this happen? I still feel like I'm just starting out, still the angry outsider—though as my wife recently recently pointed out, anyone whose work has repeatedly appeared on the op-ed page of the *New York Times* is hardly an upstart. Not that I don't have mixed feelings about *that*. I've spent most of my career on the fringes, and frankly that suits me just fine. I'm comfortable on the margins, not in your face so much as seeping slowly into your consciousness, like a contaminated water table gradually working its way toward the surface. My forays into the belly of the mainstream beast have been occasionally rewarding, but more often disastrous—some of you may remember how quickly I was fired from *U.S. News & World Report,* and though I was slated to be a regular contributor to *Brill's Content,* Steve Brill put the lid on that one five minutes after reading my first submission, a piece which mildly suggested a correlation between the bias of the media and the biases of the media's ownership—a thesis with which he did not agree and chose not to run, thereby proving my point. (Ironically enough, a recent article about political cartooning in *Brill's* pretty much anointed yours truly as the future of the profession.) And then there was the year I spent trying to develop animated content for a certain live weekend television program of an ostensibly humorous nature, an Alice-in-Wonderland journey mostly spent trying to protect my work from that show's base, scatological sensibility while still producing something they'd be willing to put on the air—an effort which was probably doomed from the start.

But these are just diversions, frequently frustrating, occasionally amusing. The important thing is that for "ten years" (ahem—give or take), I have had the privilege of appearing weekly in alternative papers (and a small handful of dailies) across the country, and that enough of you have paid attention that I've actually been able to carve out a livelihood doing this. There is only one conclusion to be drawn here: I am an absurdly lucky man. And don't think I don't know it. I mean, I wasn't exactly the kind of person who gets voted "most likely to succeed" in high school. I remember being called in one day to discuss my future career options with the guidance counselor, who had one of those little personality tests that you filled out with a number two pencil (this is how we did it back in grandpa's day, children), indicating your likes and dislikes, and I dutifully filled it out and he sent it in to one of the giant steam-powered computers we used in those days, and a couple of weeks later the results came back, and as it turned out, I was not qualified to do anything. Seriously. There was simply no job for which I was temperamentally suited. And during the first decade or so of my checkered working life, this was pretty much the case. I had one job when I was twenty or so, developing architectural blueprints, which involved feeding large sheets of paper into a machine which reeked of various toxic chemicals, primarily ammonia—and as if breathing ammonia fumes eight hours a day weren't fun enough, I was also relegated to the always-desirable graveyard shift, and while this may come as a surprise to those of you who are familiar with the sunny, good-natured tone of my cartoon, I had, yes, a bit of an attitude problem. In fact, I recently came across a copy of a memo issued by my employer at the time, which noted in part that "Dan has become a chronic complainer about hours and conditions," and warned of dire consequences if I did not straighten up and fly right. And in retrospect, I have to say, this was a pretty fair and insightful summary of my overall attitude, and the fortunate thing is that I was eventually able to figure out a way to get *paid* for being a chronic complainer, and I'll tell you this: it's nice work if you can get it.

Thanks, as always, are due numerous people, first and foremost Keith Kahla at St. Martin's, who fights a lot of battles so I don't have to. As for the editors who continue to run my cartoon in their papers each week (and of course to David Talbot, who keeps posting my work on that little webzine of his)—I can't possibly express the debt of gratitude I owe every single one of you. Thanks also to my Bigshot Author friend Dave for the intro; to Maureen McGowan and Steve Rhodes for sparing me the tedium of learning HTML; to Harold Moss, for his tireless enthusiasm in the ongoing attempt to animate Sparky and the gang; and yet again to Jello Biafra, this time for shoehorning me into the Spitfire tour. And all of you who read the cartoon each week, even those of you who send me e-mail picking me to pieces about one damn thing or another—I am perpetually astonished that you consider it worth the bother. Thank you.

And, a personal note: I got married last year, to a woman who eagerly embraced a honeymoon spent visiting such romantic locales as . . .

—a low budget recreation of the Holy Land in Bedford, Virginia;

—a rundown museum dedicated to the glories of capitalism in Oklahoma City, which, perversely, had almost nothing for sale in its gift shop;

—a nearly abandoned "educational" theme park from the fifties featuring imaginatively painted, life-sized concrete-and-rebar dinosaurs in Eureka Springs, Arkansas;

—that same city's extraordinary Passion Play, an Ed-Wood-on-Broadway Biblical extravaganza;

—and of course, the International UFO Museum and Research Center in Roswell, New Mexico . . .

. . . and who even remained good-humored when her husband insisted on driving hundreds of miles out of the way in order to sleep in a motel room shaped like a wigwam, and if that's not reason enough to dedicate this book to her, the countless ideas I have stolen from her and passed off as my own probably are. So this one's for Beverly, as is everything I do.

Dan Perkins
(Tom Tomorrow)
May 2000

THIS MODERN WORLD

by TOM TOMORROW

THIS WEEK: A *GENERIC TOM TOMORROW CARTOON*, APPLICABLE TO *ANY BREAKING NEWS STORY* THAT MAY OCCUR DURING TOM'S CURRENT *VACATION!*

MISGUIDED ENTHUSIASM FOR SOCIAL TREND OR POLITICAL EVENT BASED ON UNCRITICAL ACCEPTANCE OF SUPERFICIAL MAINSTREAM NEWS COVERAGE!

CASTIGATION OF MISGUIDED ENTHUSIASM--

--FOLLOWED BY ALTERNATE ANALYSIS OF TREND OR EVENT ROOTED IN A MORE CYNICAL VIEW OF THE PROBABLE THOUGH UNSTATED MOTIVES OF THE POLITICIANS OR OTHER PROTAGONISTS INVOLVED!

UNCOMFORTABLE PAUSE.

DECLARATION OF CONTINUED ENTHUSIASM FOR TREND OR EVENT, AND/OR REITERATION OF FAITH IN CONVENTIONAL WISDOM!

RESIGNED SIGH, ACKNOWLEDGING THAT ALTERNATIVE ANALYSIS IS UNLIKELY TO GAIN WIDESPREAD ACCEPTANCE.

THIS MODERN WORLD--THE CARTOON THAT ALWAYS STAYS ON TOP OF THE NEWS, EVEN WHEN IT DOESN'T!

TOM TOMORROW© 2000 ... tomorrow@well.com ... www.thismodernworld.com

1

THIS MODERN WORLD

by TOM TOMORROW

IMAGINE, IF YOU WILL, AN INFINITE NUMBER OF *PARALLEL UNIVERSES*--EACH *NEARLY* IDENTICAL TO OUR OWN, YET STRANGELY *DIVERGENT*...UNIVERSES WHERE THIS CARTOON FEATURES AN *AUK* RATHER THAN A *PENGUIN*...OR WHERE THE *SPICE GIRLS* PROMOTE *COKE* INSTEAD OF *PEPSI*...

WEIRD, HUH?

NOW, IMAGINE THAT RESIDENTS OF ONE UNIVERSE ARE SOMETIMES UNWITTINGLY *TRANSPOSED* WITH THEIR COUNTERPARTS IN ANOTHER! MOST THINGS WOULD *LOOK* THE SAME TO THESE ACCIDENTAL TOURISTS-- YET THEY WOULD POSSESS MEMORIES OF EVENTS WHICH *HAD NOT OCCURRED* IN THEIR PRESENT UNIVERSE!

THIS COULD EXPLAIN A *LOT* ABOUT THE CLINTON WHITE HOUSE...

FOR INSTANCE, CONSIDER *GARY ALDRICH* --THE FORMER FBI AGENT WHO CLAIMS TO HAVE SEEN HILLARY CLINTON DECORATING THE WHITE HOUSE CHRISTMAS TREE WITH SEXUAL AND DRUG-RELATED PARAPHERNALIA...AND MAYBE HE *DID*-- IN SOME *PARALLEL UNIVERSE*...

COME ON, GARY! HELP US HANG THESE CRACK PIPES AND CONDOMS ON THE TREE! IT'S GOING TO BE A DEGENERATE LIBERAL CHRISTMAS AROUND *HERE*! HEH, HEH!

OH MY GOD! I'VE GOT TO WARN THE *AMERICAN PEOPLE*!

OR--ON THE OTHER HAND--CONSIDER THE PRESIDENT *HIMSELF*...PERHAPS HIS INABILITY TO ADEQUATELY EXPLAIN HIS RELATIONSHIP WITH MONICA LEWINSKY IS DUE TO THE FACT THAT THERE REALLY *WASN'T* ONE-- IN HIS UNIVERSE OF *ORIGIN*, AT LEAST...

MIKE, I'M COMPLETELY BAFFLED HERE! CAN'T WE JUST EXPLAIN TO EVERYONE THAT I'M A HAPPILY-MARRIED, CHURCHGOING MAN WHO'S NEVER LOOKED *TWICE* AT ANOTHER WOMAN?

HEE, HEE, HEE! GOOD ONE, SIR!

BUT SERIOUSLY, WHAT DO YOU WANT US TO DO?

OF COURSE, IT'S IMPORTANT TO REMEMBER THAT THIS IS JUST A *THEORY*.

WELL IT CERTAINLY SOUNDS PLAUSIBLE TO ME!

I THINK IT IS A MAJOR BREAKTHROUGH IN SCIENTIFIC UNDERSTANDING!

TOM TOMORROW DESERVES A *NOBEL PRIZE* IF YOU ASK ME...

2

THIS MODERN WORLD
by TOM TOMORROW

WITH MOVIES LIKE *PRIMARY COLORS* AND *WAG THE DOG* MIRRORING REAL-LIFE POLITICS, WE SEEM TO HAVE ENTERED A PHASE OF *LIFE* IMITATING ART IMITATING *LIFE*...

WHAT ARE YOU WATCHING--THE *NEWS*--OR *ENTERTAINMENT TONIGHT*?

UH--I'M NOT ACTUALLY *SURE*...

UNFORTUNATELY, HOWEVER, *REALITY* HAS BEEN FULL OF LUDICROUS PLOT TWISTS NO SELF-RESPECTING SCREENWRITER WOULD *CONSIDER* USING... FOR INSTANCE, WHAT SITTING PRESIDENT WITH A REPUTATION FOR PHILANDERING AND A THEN-IMPENDING SEXUAL HARASSMENT LAWSUIT WOULD EVEN *THINK* ABOUT DOING WHAT BILL CLINTON IS ALLEGED TO HAVE DONE?

I DON'T CARE IF I AM THE MOST POWERFUL MAN IN THE WORLD! I'D GIVE IT ALL UP IN A *MINUTE*--

--IN ORDER TO HAVE SEX WITH THAT MODERATELY ATTRACTIVE, BIG-HAIRED INTERN!

AND WHAT REAL-LIFE PROSECUTOR, ALREADY DERIDED FOR HIS McCARTHY-LIKE TACTICS, WOULD RISK SETTING OFF A CIVIL LIBERTIES *UPROAR* BY SUBPEONAING A BOOKSTORE'S SALES RECORDS--TO FIND OUT WHAT THE INTERN HAS BEEN *READING*?

"THE JOY OF SEX WITH BILL CLINTON"... "TEN HABITS OF HIGHLY EFFECTIVE PEOPLE WHO LIE TO GRAND JURIES"...

HAH! I KNEW WE'D FIND A SMOKING GUN SOMEWHERE!

SO...AS LONG AS WE SEEM TO BE STUCK WITH THE SPECTACLE OF POLITICS AS *ENTERTAINMENT*--WELL-- CAN'T WE AT LEAST GET SOME *DECENT SCRIPTS*..?

HERE'S LOOKING AT YOU, KID! WE'LL ALWAYS HAVE *WASHINGTON*!

THE FLOOR OF THE OVAL OFFICE, ANYWAY!

SOMEONE HAS HAD SEX WITH THE PRESIDENT!

...ROUND UP THE USUAL SUSPECTS.

TOM TOMORROW © 4-15-98

3

THIS MODERN WORLD

by TOM TOMORROW

THIS IS TRUE: A HIGH SCHOOL IN EVANS, GA., RECENTLY HELD A SPECIAL "COKE IN EDUCATION" DAY-- AS PART OF AN EFFORT TO WIN A $500 PRIZE FROM THE COCA COLA COMPANY...*

$500!? WHY, THEIR GENEROSITY IS SURPASSED ONLY BY THEIR EXPERTISE IN PRODUCING DELICIOUS CARBONATED BEVERAGES!

YES--THAT'S ALMOST ENOUGH TO BUY EACH OF OUR STUDENTS A REFRESHING, ICE COLD CAN OF COCA COLA-- AMERICA'S FAVORITE SOFT DRINK!

*AND, TO BE FAIR, A SHOT AT A $10,000 NATIONAL PRIZE. BUT STILL...

ACCORDING TO A.P., THE SCHOOL "INVITED A COKE MARKETING EXECUTIVE TO ADDRESS ECONOMICS STUDENTS, HAD CHEMISTRY STUDENTS ANALYZE THE SUGAR CONTENT OF COKE, AND USED A COCA-COLA CAKE RECIPE IN HOME ECONOMICS..."

SO WHAT HAVE WE LEARNED TODAY, CHILDREN?

UM--COKE HAS A LOT OF SUGAR...

...AND CAN BE USED AS AN INGREDIENT IN SICKLY SWEET BAKED GOODS!

VERY GOOD!

HOWEVER...TWO YOUNG REBELS APPARENTLY DISRUPTED THE DAY'S EVENTS-- AND RUINED A SCHOOL PICTURE IN WHICH STUDENTS SPELLED OUT THE WORD "COKE"-- BY WEARING PEPSI SHIRTS!

YOU MINDLESS SHEEP DISGUST ME! I AM AN INDIVIDUAL-- A NONCONFORMIST-- --A PEPSI DRINKER!

THIS IS EXACTLY WHAT OUR FOREFATHERS HAD IN MIND WHEN THEY WROTE THE FIRST AMENDMENT, YOU KNOW!

FORTUNATELY, SCHOOL OFFICIALS QUICKLY DISCIPLINED THE BOYS... AFTER ALL, YOU NEVER KNOW WHAT KIND OF TROUBLE MIGHT BE CAUSED BY SOMEONE WEARING THE WRONG COLORS TO SCHOOL...

YO, WASSUP? YOU DOWN WITH THE BIG C?

GOT THAT RIGHT, CUZ! I'M CHILLIN' WITH THE REAL THING!

WORD! LET'S FIND THOSE PEPSI BOYS AND BUST SOME HEADS!

TOM TOMORROW ©4-22-98

4

THIS MODERN WORLD

by TOM TOMORROW

IT'S TIME FOR ANOTHER EXCERPT FROM THE TRAVEL JOURNALS OF *SPARKY THE PENGUIN!* THIS WEEK: SPARKY GOES TO THE *WHITE HOUSE CORRESPONDENTS' DINNER!*

WHY ARE ALL THESE PEOPLE TRYING TO LOOK LIKE ME?

"THERE IS LITTLE EVIDENCE HERE TONIGHT OF THE SUPPOSEDLY ADVERSARIAL RELATIONSHIP BETWEEN POLITICIANS AND THE MEDIA... WHEN THE PRESIDENT TAKES THE PODIUM, HE JOKES ABOUT HIS RECENT TROUBLES AS IF TALKING TO A ROOMFUL OF 2,600 *CLOSE FRIENDS*..."

I'VE BEEN SO BUSY, I HAVEN'T READ A NEWSPAPER SINCE THE *POPE* WENT TO *CUBA!*

WHAT HAVE YOU ALL BEEN *WRITING* ABOUT?

HA HA

HA HA

"OF COURSE, THIS IS LESS A POLITICAL EVENT THAN A CELEBRITY *CIRCUS*-- A SURREAL CONFLUENCE OF POLITICIANS, MOVIE STARS AND THE JOURNALISTIC ELITE, ALL MEMBERS OF AN EXCLUSIVE CLUB TO WHICH *FAME* IS THE ONLY ADMISSION REQUIREMENT... GUESTS RANGE FROM SHARON STONE TO HENRY KISSINGER TO GORDON LIDDY TO JON BON JOVI--"

HELLO I'M FAMOUS!

PLEASED TO MEET YOU! I'M FAMOUS AS WELL!

"--TO *PAULA JONES,* WHO IS APPARENTLY TRYING TO PARLAY HER FIFTEEN MINUTES OF FAME INTO A CAREER AS A TEAM *MASCOT* FOR THE FAR RIGHT--SORT OF A *PHILLY PHANATIC* FOR THE ANTI-CLINTON CONTINGENT..."

GO-O-O-O **TEAM!!**

"AFTER THE DINNER, COCKTAIL PARTIES ABOUND... WITH PREENING, STATUS-CONSCIOUS ATTENDEES DISTRACTEDLY PRETENDING TO CONVERSE WHILE CONTINUOUSLY SCANNING THE CROWD OVER EACH OTHERS' *SHOULDERS*..."

KIND OF LIKE A HIGH SCHOOL PROM--EXCEPT THAT SAM *DONALDSON* IS ONE OF THE COOL KIDS...

UM, YES, I AGREE--WAR IS BAD...

SAY--IS THAT PAULA!?

"IN THIS CROWD, IT REALLY DOESN'T MATTER WHAT SOMEONE HAS DONE TO *BECOME* FAMOUS--JUST THAT THEY *ARE FAMOUS*... CONTEXT IS *IRRELEVANT* AT THE WHITE HOUSE CORRESPONDENTS' DINNER, WHILE SHAMELESS SUPERFICIALITY IS THE *DOMINANT MOTIF*..."

--WHICH, OF COURSE, PRETTY MUCH SUMS UP WHITE HOUSE CORRESPONDENTS *THEMSELVES*...

OH, WHO CARES WHAT *YOU* THINK?

YOU'VE NEVER BEEN ON TELEVISION!

TOM TOMORROW © 5-20-98

THIS MODERN WORLD

by TOM TOMORROW

IF YOU BELIEVE THAT A FREE-MARKET INSURANCE SYSTEM MAKES *SENSE*...

WELL OF *COURSE* A PARASITICAL MIDDLE-MAN HAS TO MAKE A PROFIT BEFORE I CAN BE ALLOWED ACCESS TO HEALTH CARE!

IT'S THE AMERICAN WAY!

IF YOU BELIEVE THAT HEALTH INSURANCE *SHOULD* BE INEXTRICABLY LINKED TO EMPLOYMENT STATUS...

IF THOSE SELF-EMPLOYED PEOPLE WANTED TO BE ABLE TO SEE *DOCTORS*--

--THEY SHOULD HAVE GOTTEN *NORMAL* JOBS-- LIKE THE *REST* OF US!

IF YOU BELIEVE THAT THE CANADIAN SINGLE-PAYER SYSTEM IS SOME SORT OF *COMMUNIST PLOT*...

YOU KNOW-- IT ACTUALLY SOUNDS LIKE A PRETTY *SENSIBLE* SOLUTION...

HEY--YOU WATCH YOUR MOUTH, CANADA-LOVER! WE DON'T GO FOR THAT KIND OF TALK HERE IN THE *U.S. OF A!*

More Doctors Smoke CAMELS than any other cigarette!

Shot and a beer $1.50

...THEN I GUESS YOU GET THE HEALTH CARE SYSTEM YOU *DESERVE.*

SURE, I HAVE TO WAIT FIVE WEEKS FOR AN APPOINTMENT WITH MY OFFICIALLY-DESIGNATED *PRIMARY CARE PROVIDER*-- WHO THEN REFERS ME TO A *SPECIALIST* WHO CAN'T SEE ME FOR *ANOTHER* FIVE WEEKS--

--BUT AT LEAST I DON'T HAVE TO DEAL WITH SOME *GOVERNMENT BUREAUCRACY!*

YES, WHAT A NIGHTMARE *THAT* WOULD BE...

TOM TOMORROW © 6-3-98

THIS MODERN WORLD

by TOM TOMORROW

BIG SUMMER MOVIES ARE TO POLITICAL CARTOONISTS WHAT BIG-HAIRED WO-MEN ARE TO BILL CLINTON... AND THIS YEAR, WE SUSPECT FEW CARTOON-ISTS WILL BE ABLE TO RE-SIST THE LURE OF THAT MOST BLUNT OF VISUAL MET-APHORS--

--GODZILLA...

I TELL YOU--SMALL ENTREPRENEURS JUST DON'T HAVE A *CHANCE* AGAINST *MICROSOFT!*

ER--I THINK YOU MAY BE IN THE WRONG CARTOON--*WE* REPRESENT SMALL DEPOSITORS COPING WITH GIANT BANK MERGERS!

WAIT--I THOUGHT WE WERE *HMO PATIENTS!*

ALSO, IF THE FORTHCOMING *X-FILES* MOVIE IS A HIT, WE'RE LIKELY TO SEE A SUCCESSION OF EDITORIAL CARTOONS FEATURING *KEN STARR* AS *MULDER*--AND MAYBE *LINDA TRIPP* AS *SCULLY...*

I'M CONFUSED--DOES THIS MEAN MONICA LEWINSKY IS AN EVIL, SHAPE-SHIFTING *ALIEN* BENT ON *WORLD DOM-INATION?*

IT'S PROBABLY BEST NOT TO STRETCH THE ANALOGY TOO FAR.

SEX FILES

FBI

FBI

AND THEN THERE'S *BULWORTH*...THIS ONE MAY OR MAY NOT TAKE OFF IN THE MAINSTREAM--BUT YOU CAN *BET* YOU'LL SEE OBVIOUS PARALLELS BEING DRAWN IN MORE THAN ONE SO-CALLED "ALTERNATIVE" CARTOON...*

THEY CALL ME BILLY CEE AND I'M HERE TO SAY YO--IF YOU WANT ACCESS TO *ME* YOU BETTER COUGH UP SOME *DOUGH!*

WORD!

GO, MACK DADDY!

*INCLUDING THIS ONE, OF COURSE.

TOM TOMORROW © 5-27-98

THIS MODERN WORLD

by TOM TOMORROW

"The guns taken from accused shooter Kip Kinkel were a .22 caliber Ruger semiautomatic rifle and two semiautomatic pistols: a 9mm Glock and a .22 Ruger ... Such guns were not included in the 1994 federal ban on assault weapons. Lawmakers concluded that a .22 isn't powerful enough to do significant damage." -- *Associated Press*

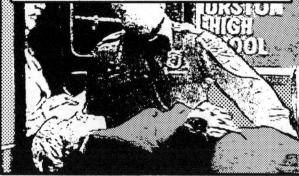

"Springfield's tragedy is only the latest in an appalling spate of school-related shootings in recent months. Since Oct. 1, when a distraught 16-year-old allegedly shot nine fellow students in Pearl, Miss., 14 people have been killed and 26 have been wounded in eight separate incidents, including the playground massacre in Jonesboro, Ark. on March 24." -- *Newsweek*

"When I snap, I want the firepower to kill people." -- *Kip Kinkel to high school friend.*

"I just like guns." -- *Kinkel to Springfield police after being detained for possession of a stolen pistol the day before the shooting.*

"(It's important) not to make guns the issue." -- *Robert Ryker, father of wounded student Jake Ryker and staunch N.R.A. supporter.*

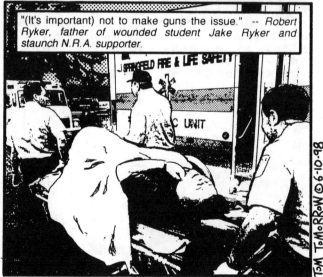

8

THIS MODERN WORLD

by TOM TOMORROW

THE CONSTITUTIONAL AMENDMENT TO PROHIBIT FLAG BURNING WAS PASSED BY THE HOUSE LAST YEAR, AND IS EXPECTED TO COME UP FOR A VOTE IN THE SENATE THIS SUMMER OR FALL... SO ONCE AGAIN, AMERICANS MUST DEBATE THIS *VERY IMPORTANT ISSUE*...

IT IS THE MOST URGENT DILEMMA FACING OUR NATION TODAY!

I CAN BARELY SLEEP AT NIGHT, SO GREAT IS MY CONCERN!

WE HAVE TO ADMIT, IT'S *QUITE A PROBLEM!* WHY, YOU CAN BARELY WALK OUT THE FRONT DOOR THESE DAYS WITHOUT RUNNING INTO SOMEONE *BURNING A FLAG*...

DARN IT--THIS CHARCOAL JUST WON'T *CATCH!*

HEY, NO PROBLEM, BILL! JUST THROW ON THIS *AMERICAN FLAG!*

AS FAR AS *WE'RE* CONCERNED, RESPECT MUST BE SHOWN FOR THE FLAG IN *ANY REPRESENTATION*--

HOLD IT RIGHT THERE, BUB! IF YOU MAIL THAT LETTER, THAT *FLAG STAMP* WILL BE *DESECRATED* BY THE POST OFFICE'S CANCELLATION MARK!

I--I DIDN'T REALIZE--

I'LL LET YOU OFF THIS TIME--BUT *DON'T LET IT HAPPEN AGAIN!*

--INCLUDING *THIS* ONE...SO DON'T YOU DARE TOSS THIS CARTOON IN THE RECYCLING BIN-- UNLESS YOU'RE SOME KIND OF *GODLESS COMMIE*, THAT IS...

UM, I GUESS WE'D BETTER CUT IT OUT AND KEEP IT ON THE REFRIGERATOR...FOR THE REST OF OUR *LIVES*...

I DON'T SEE ANY OTHER OPTION!

TOM TOMORROW © 6-17-98

THIS MODERN WORLD

by TOM TOMORROW

IT BEGINS WITH AN ONSLAUGHT OF JOURNALISTIC PUFF PIECES--EVEN IN MAGAZINES SUPPOSEDLY DEDICATED TO COVERING THE *NEWS*...

TIME

Newsweek

Esqu

Leo DiCaprio stretches his wings as a talking penguin -- but will the movie fly?

THIS MODERN WORLD
THE MOVIE!

Cartoonist whines about script -- no one cares

TANTALIZING PLOT REVELATIONS ARE SLOWLY LEAKED IN ORDER TO WHET THE PUBLIC'S *APPETITE*...

I HEARD THAT SPARKY MAY NOT BE A PENGUIN AT ALL--BUT RATHER AN *AUK*!

THAT WOULD BE A SHOCKING PLOT TWIST! AFTER ALL-- NO ONE CARES WHAT AN *AUK* HAS TO SAY!

AT LAST, THE BIG DAY ARRIVES ARRIVES...EAGER ENTERTAINMENT CONSUMERS ACROSS THE NATION RUSH OFF TO THEIR LOCAL MEGAPLEXES...

THIS IS ALMOST CERTAIN TO BE ONE OF THE FINEST MOTION PICTURES *EVER MADE*! WHY, THEY SPENT HUNDREDS OF MILLIONS OF DOLLARS ON THE SPECIAL EFFECTS *ALONE*!

YES--AND THE SOUNDTRACK FEATURES THE MUSIC OF *MANY* CURRENTLY POPULAR BANDS!

...AND SLOWLY REALIZE THAT ONCE AGAIN, THEY'VE BEEN HAD.

MAN, THAT SUCKED.

BUT LOOK! THE "FAMILY CIRCUS" MOVIE IS OPENING IN THREE WEEKS-- WITH *MATT DAMON* AS *LITTLE BILLY*!

LET'S GO SEE IF THERE'S A NEWSMAGAZINE COVER STORY WE CAN READ IN THE MEANTIME!

TOM TOMORROW © 6-24-98

10

THIS MODERN WORLD

by TOM TOMORROW

THIS MODERN WORLD

by TOM TOMORROW

THIS WEEK: NRA SPOKESGUN *SNUB-NOSED SAM* SPEAKS WITH NEW NRA PRESIDENT *CHARLTON HESTON!*

CHUCK, YOU'VE SAID SCHOOLYARD SHOOTINGS ARE "A CHILD ISSUE, NOT A GUN ISSUE." *

THAT'S TRUE, SAM... SINCE THE SHOOTERS ARE ALMOST ALWAYS *TROUBLED BOYS*--

*ACTUAL QUOTE

--THERE'S CLEARLY JUST *ONE* SOLUTION HERE...THE CRIMINALIZATION OF *AWKWARD BEHAVIOR* IN ADOLESCENT *MALES!*

HMMM... SO AT THE FIRST SIGN OF *SHYNESS* OR *INTROVERSION* IN A TEENAGE BOY--

--LOCK HIM UP AND THROW AWAY THE KEY! PROBLEM SOLVED! END OF STORY!

THERE'S *NOTHING ELSE* SOCIETY CAN *POSSIBLY* DO!

WELL, THEN-- I GUESS THAT WRAPS US UP FOR THIS WEEK! JOIN US NEXT TIME WHEN WE'LL DISCUSS YOUR INALIENABLE RIGHT TO A *SURFACE-TO-AIR MISSILE LAUNCHER!*

SO YOU WANT TO GO POP OFF A FEW AT THE SHOOTING RANGE?

I THOUGHT YOU'D NEVER ASK, BIG FELLA!

TOM TOMORROW © 8-5-98

CLIP-N-SAVE BONUS PANEL: CHARLTON HESTON'S REASONS *YOU* SHOULD OWN A GUN (NO. 37 IN A SERIES)!

--BECAUSE YOU NEVER KNOW WHEN SOME DAMN DIRTY APE WILL TRY TO PUT HIS STINKING PAWS ON *YOU!*

SORRY MR. HESTON! WE MISTOOK YOU FOR AN EASILY VICTIMIZED *NON GUN OWNER!*

IT WON'T HAPPEN AGAIN!

13

THIS MODERN WORLD

by TOM TOMORROW

Biff: LOOK AT THIS, WANDA! TIME MAGAZINE HAS POSED THE PROVOCATIVE QUESTION: "IS FEMINISM *DEAD?*"

YOU'RE A GAL! WHAT DO *YOU* THINK?

Wanda: WELL, *BIFF*...I THINK THAT WHAT TIME IS CRITIQUING HERE IS NOT *FEMINISM* SO MUCH AS THE *PORTRAYAL* OF FEMINISM IN MAIN-STREAM PUBLICATIONS SUCH AS--WELL--*TIME*...

...A MAGAZINE, INCIDENTALLY, WHERE ONLY THREE OUT OF ELEVEN SENIOR EDITORS-- AND TWO OUT OF *TWENTY-TWO* SENIOR WRITERS-- ACTUALLY *ARE*, UM, GALS...*

...I ALSO THINK IT'S *LUDICROUS* THAT TIME HAS CHOSEN *ALLY McBEAL*-- A FICTIONAL TV CHARACTER, FOR CHRISSAKES-- TO REPRESENT CONTEMPORARY FEMINISM ON ITS *COVER*...

IT REALLY MAKES ME WONDER IF SOCIETY WILL *EVER* TAKE WOMEN SERIOUSLY-- OR IF WE'LL ALWAYS BE SUBJECT TO THESE *PATRONIZING STEREOTYPES*...YOU KNOW, WE'RE EITHER MAN-HATING *BRA BURNERS* OR WE'RE DITZY, SELF-INVOLVED *FLUFFHEADS*--

Wanda: BIFF, WHY ARE YOU LOOKING AT ME LIKE THAT?

Biff: OH--I'M SORRY! YOU'RE JUST SO DARNED *CUTE* WHEN YOU GET RILED UP! WHAT WERE YOU SAYING ABOUT *BURNING* YOUR BRA?

SIGH...I DON'T KNOW WHY I EVEN *BOTHER*...

TOM TOMORROW © 7-15-98 *TIP OF THE PEN TO KATHA POLLITT

14

THIS MODERN WORLD

by TOM TOMORROW

CRUSADING FOR JUSTICE AS ONLY THEY ARE ABLE...IT'S--

THE ANNOYING DUO!

ANAGRAM MAN!

SONG-IN-YOUR-HEAD BOY!

LATE AT NIGHT IN WASHINGTON D.C., SENATOR TRENT LOTT SCHEMES TO DEFEAT ANOTHER ROUND OF CAMPAIGN FINANCE REFORM PROPOSALS...

WE'LL FRAME IT AS A CIVIL RIGHTS ISSUE...AFTER ALL--heh heh--THE POOR HAVE AS MUCH RIGHT TO CONTRIBUTE AS THE RICH!

HOLD IT RIGHT THERE, SENATOR!

WHAT--?

CRASH!

ANAGRAM MAN LEADS THE CHARGE!

HARD TO DO YOUR CORPORATE MASTERS' BIDDING WHEN SOMEONE IS MAKING SILLY ANAGRAMS OUT OF YOUR NAME, ISN'T IT SENATOR TRENT LOTT--

--OR SHOULD I SAY-- ROTTEN TALENT ROTS?!

YOU KNOW, THAT IS ANNOYING!

HIS YOUTHFUL SIDEKICK SONG-IN-YOUR-HEAD BOY THEN DELIVERS THE KNOCKOUT PUNCH!

BORN FREE, SENATOR... AS FREE AS THE WIND BLOWS...

NO! STOP! I'LL NEVER GET THAT TUNE OUT OF MY HEAD!

...AS FREE AS THE GRASS GROWS...AAARGH!

SENATOR LOTT WON'T BE GETTING ANY MORE WORK DONE TONIGHT, SONG-IN-YOUR-HEAD BOY!

IT'S ANOTHER INCREMENTAL VICTORY FOR THE ANNOYING DUO, ANAGRAM MAN!

PERHAPS WE SHOULD PAY THE PRESIDENT A VISIT...I THINK THE THEME FROM JEOPARDY MIGHT KEEP HIM DISTRACTED FOR A FEW HOURS...

TOM TOMORROW©7-22-98

15

THIS MODERN WORLD

by TOM TOMORROW

THIS MODERN WORLD

by TOM TOMORROW

THE PRESIDENT HAS A MEETING WITH HIS *HOLLY-WOOD BACKERS*...

BILL, YOU KNOW WE'VE GIVEN YOU A LOT OF HELP.

IT'S TIME TO RE-TURN THE FAVOR.

"WAG THE DOG" IS OUT ON VIDEO-- AND WE NEED TO CREATE SOME SORT OF *BUZZ*.

HERE'S THE PLAN: YOU CONFESS TO YOUR AFFAIR WITH MONICA-- AND THEN FIND AN EXCUSE TO *BOMB SOME-BODY!*

BUT-- THEN PEOPLE WILL THINK I'M TRYING TO *DIS-TRACT* THEM FROM THE *SCAN-DAL*--

EXACTLY! THE "WAG THE DOG" SCENARIO WILL BE ON *EVERYONE'S* LIPS--

--AND OUR SALES WILL SHOOT THROUGH THE *ROOF!* WHADDYA SAY, BIG GUY?

WELL-- CAN YOU CUT ME IN FOR A PIECE OF THE *GROSS?*

HEY-- YOU'VE GOT *YOUR* CONSPIRACY THEORIES... AND WE'VE GOT *OURS*...

©'98 TOM TOMORROW-- WITH A HUGE TIP O' THE PEN TO JASON VEST--

17

THIS MODERN WORLD

by TOM TOMORROW

NOW THAT THE SECRET SERVICE HAS BEEN COMPELLED TO TESTIFY, CLINTON APOLOGISTS WORRY THAT THE PRESIDENT'S ABILITY TO LEAD THE NATION HAS BEEN PERMANENTLY *COMPROMISED*.

IT IS AN OUT- RAGE!

HOW CAN HE *GOVERN* IF HE IS NOT FREE TO MAKE UNSAVORY BACK- ROOM DEALS SAFE FROM THE PRYING EYES OF THE *VOTING PUBLIC*?

OF COURSE, GIVEN THAT THE PRESIDENT IS NOT A TOTALITARIAN *DICTATOR* -- BUT RATHER, THE ELECTED REPRESENTATIVE OF AN OSTENSIBLY OPEN, *DEMOCRATIC SOCIETY* -- WELL, *WE'RE* NOT CONVINCED THAT *INCREASED ACCOUNTABILITY* WOULD BE SUCH A *TERRIBLE THING*...

ACCORDING TO OUR RESEARCH, TOSSING *HOMELESS ORPHANS* OFF *WELFARE* WILL BOOST YOUR RATINGS BY AT LEAST *THREE POINTS*!

THAT'S GREAT!

--UH--BUT IT WOULD BE WRONG.

AHEM.

MAYBE WE SHOULD TAKE THINGS A STEP *FURTHER*...FOR INSTANCE, THERE'D BE NO NEED FOR *CAMPAIGN FINANCE REFORM* IF MEMBERS OF CONGRESS KNEW THAT *ANYTHING THEY DID* WOULD SOON BE A MATTER OF *PUBLIC RECORD*...

I CAN'T ACCEPT A CONTRIBUTION FROM AN INDUSTRY WHICH HAS LEGISLATION PEND- ING IN THE SENATE! THAT WOULD BE UN- *ETHICAL*!

BUT--BUT WE ALWAYS--

THAT'S ENOUGH OUT OF YOU! GUARDS! REMOVE THIS MAN!

IN FACT, MAYBE WE SHOULD FOLLOW THE EXAMPLE OF THAT YOUNG WOMAN WHO BROADCASTS HER ENTIRE LIFE ON THE INTERNET-- AND SET UP "JENNICAMS" TO FOLLOW EVERY ELECTED REP- RESENTATIVE, *TWENTY FOUR HOURS A DAY*!

TO *HELL* WITH THE MONIED IN- TERESTS, GENTLE- MEN! WE ARE HERE TO SERVE THE *AMERICAN PEOPLE*!

YES--THAT'S *ALWAYS* BEEN *MY* PRIMARY CONCERN!

WHAT--? OH...YEAH, YEAH... ME TOO...

SIGH...

NUDGE NUDGE

ARMEY

LOTT

TOM TOMORROW © 8-19-98

THIS MODERN WORLD

by TOM TOMORROW

WHAT THE WHITE HOUSE PRESS CORPS DOESN'T SEEM TO UNDERSTAND--

MIKE, DID THE PRESIDENT HAVE ANY REACTION TO THE LATEST NEWS FROM KEN STARR'S OFFICE?

--IS THAT SOON-TO-RETIRE PRESS SECRETARY MIKE McCURRY ISN'T JUST AN ENIGMATICALLY EVASIVE FLACK--

SAM, THE PRESIDENT BELIEVES HE HAS HEARD THE SOUND OF ONE HAND CLAPPING--

--AND HE HAS NO FURTHER COMMENT.

--BUT RATHER, A HIGHLY-EVOLVED MASTER OF ZEN BUDDHISM--

ER, MIKE-- COULD YOU CLARIFY THAT FOR US?

LET ME PUT IT THIS WAY, SAM--A DUCK MAY GAZE UPON THE BUDDHA--BUT HE STILL WILL NOT EAT RADISHES!

--WHO'S SPENT THE PAST FEW YEARS PATIENTLY TRYING TO GUIDE THEM TOWARDS ENLIGHTENMENT!

I DON'T UNDERSTAND.

I CAN LEAD YOU TO WATER, SAM-- BUT I CANNOT MAKE YOU PLAY THE VIOLIN.

GO NOW, AND PONDER.

THIS MODERN WORLD

by TOM TOMORROW

JUST A THOUGHT...BUT WOULD CONGRESS HAVE BEEN ABLE TO POST THE SEXUALLY EXPLICIT STARR REPORT ON THE NET IF THE *COMMUNICATIONS DECENCY ACT* HADN'T BEEN RULED *UNCONSTITUTIONAL*?

WHAT KIND OF SICKO *ARE* YOU, SENATOR LOTT? THERE ARE *KIDS* ONLINE!

BUT--BUT I WAS JUST FULFILLING MY *PUBLIC DUTY*!

TELL IT TO THE JUDGE YOU BIG *PREEV*!

AT ANY RATE, THE REPORT HAS PRETTY MUCH ESTABLISHED BILL CLINTON'S PLACE IN HISTORY ALONGSIDE OTHER FAMOUS PRESIDENTIAL PREVARICATORS...

I SUBVERTED THE CONSTITUTION IN AN ATTEMPT TO SECURE MY HOLD ON *POWER!*

I SUBVERTED THE CONSTITUTION IN ORDER TO FUND MY ILLEGAL, UNDECLARED WAR IN CENTRAL AMERICA!

I LET AN INTERN PLAY WITH MY WEE-WEE!

...FOR BETTER OR WORSE...

OF COURSE, THE COMEBACK KID MAY YET FIND A WAY TO SALVAGE HIS PRESIDENCY...ESPECIALLY IF HE CAN ASSEMBLE THE RIGHT TEAM OF *EXPERTS* TO HELP HIM THROUGH THE CRISIS...

YA GOTTA DO SOME *WEEPIN'*, BILLY BOY! THAT'S THE TRICK! LET THEM TEARS *FLOW!*

THANKS, REV. SWAGGART!-- LISTEN, I'VE GOT HUGH *GRANT* ON THE OTHER LINE--

MR. PRESIDENT-- JIM BAKKER IS HERE TO SEE YOU!

WHATEVER HAPPENS, IT'S GOING TO BE A TAWDRY COUPLE OF MONTHS...ALTHOUGH--TO LOOK ON THE BRIGHT SIDE*--MAYBE THE STARR REPORT WILL AT LEAST SPELL THE END OF THE OBNOXIOUS *CIGAR CRAZE*...

SIGH...I JUST CAN'T PUT ONE OF THESE THINGS IN MY MOUTH ANYMORE WITHOUT THINKING OF--

AHEM! YES, YES...I KNOW...

*WHICH WE ALWAYS DO!

THIS MODERN WORLD

by TOM TOMORROW

THE SUMMER OF '98 DRAWS TO A CLOSE--AND NOT A MOMENT TOO SOON FOR SOME OF US...

I'M SICK OF EVERYTHING!

I'M SICK OF STEPHEN GLASS, SARIN GAS, THE Y2K GLITCH, AND THE DOW JONES AVERAGE! I'M SICK OF MAUREEN DOWD, I'M SICK OF BILL GATES, AND I'M SICK OF FAWNING ARTICLES ABOUT THE TRUE MEANING OF *SAVING PRIVATE RYAN!*

I'M SICK OF KEN STARR'S PUDGY LITTLE FACE AND I'M SICK OF THE PRESIDENT AND HIS PENIS! I'M SICK OF LINDA TRIPP'S *HAIR*, LUCIANNE GOLDBERG'S *RASP*, AND MATT DRUDGE'S *SMIRK*--

--AND I'M *REALLY* SICK OF THE SEMEN-STAINED DRESS!

I'M SICK OF TRENT LOTT! I'M SICK OF ALLY McBEAL! I'M SICK OF TIME, NEWSWEEK, THE FOX NEWS CHANNEL *AND* BRILL'S CONTENT! I'M SICK OF DICK MORRIS, GINGER SPICE, JOKES ABOUT VIAGRA, AND THE TOP-100 LIST OF *ANYTHING!*

BUT MOST OF ALL, I AM SICK, SICK, *SICK* OF THE MOST FREQUENTLY INVOKED SIX SYLLABLE NAME IN HUMAN *HISTORY--*

MON-I-CA LEW-IN-SKY!

WEATHER'S GOT *YOU* A LITTLE CRANKY, I SEE.

I'M NOT CUT OUT FOR THIS! I'M A *PENGUIN* FOR GOD'S SAKE!

21

THIS MODERN WORLD

by TOM TOMORROW

WELCOME TO FABULOUS *WALL STREET U.S.A!*

COME ON IN! OUR STAFF OF HIGHLY-TRAINED FINANCIAL EXPERTS WILL BE *GLAD* TO HELP YOU CHOOSE THE *INVESTMENT STRATEGY* THAT'S RIGHT FOR YOU!

I'M GOING TO BET MY ENTIRE RETIREMENT FUND ON RED 23!

A VERY WISE MOVE, SIR! I'M SURE YOU WON'T REGRET IT!

AND WHY NOT TAKE IN A SHOW WHILE YOU'RE HERE? OUR GORGEOUS *DANCING ECONOMISTS* CAN *ALWAYS* TALK THE MARKET UP--IF YOU KNOW WHAT WE *MEAN*...

THIS STOCK MARKET~WILL NEVER CRASH~ SO COME ON IN~AND GIVE US YOUR CASH!

SURE, YOU MAY EXPERIENCE THE OCCASIONAL SHORT *TERM LOSS*, BUT HEY-- THERE'S ALWAYS *NEXT TIME!* THE IMPORTANT THING IS TO KEEP PLAYING!

THE MARKET ALWAYS PAYS OFF IN THE LONG RUN!

YOU CAN BET YOUR ENTIRE ECONOMY ON *THAT!*

IN FACT-- YOU ALREADY HAVE!

I CAME TO WALL ST. IN A $2000 BUICK--BUT I'M LEAVING IN A $100,000 GREYHOUND BUS!

TOM TOMORROW©9-23-98

22

A NATION IN CRISIS

TOM TOMORROW'S COMPREHENSIVE GUIDE TO THE LATE UNPLEASANTNESS

...A SELF-STYLED INTERNET JOURNALIST WHO REVEALED THE DEPTH OF *HIS* HISTORICAL PERSPECTIVE IN A RECENT *PLAYBOY* INTERVIEW...

"WHO WAS PRESIDENT WHEN YOU WERE BORN?"

"IN 1966? I DON'T KNOW! THE FIRST PRESIDENT I REMEMBER WAS JIMMY CARTER!"*

SPACE FOR RENT

*ACTUAL QUOTE.

...A STRAIGHTLACED, MORALISTIC PROSECUTOR WHO'S WRITTEN WHAT MAY BE THE MOST GRATUITOUSLY SALACIOUS PUBLIC DOCUMENT IN AMERICAN *HISTORY*...

IT IS *VITALLY IMPORTANT* FOR THE PUBLIC TO KNOW THAT THE PRESIDENT MASTURBATED INTO HIS *SINK!*

UH HUH.

HOT BABES

...AND OF COURSE, THE ENIGMATIC TRIUMVIRATE OF LUCIANNE GOLDBERG, LINDA TRIPP, AND MONICA *HERSELF*...

HAVE FUN AT THE ROYAL BALL, CINDER-ELLEWINSKY!

TELL ME ALL *ABOUT* IT WHEN YOU GET BACK!

GOSH -- YOU'RE THE GREATEST STEPSISTERS *EVER!*

BOOK PROPOSAL

NOW, IT SEEMS LIKELY THAT OUR PHILANDERING, AMORAL PRESIDENT WILL SOON STAND BEFORE CONGRESS -- TO BE JUDGED BY SUCH PARAGONS OF VIRTUE AS --

--NEWT GINGRICH...WHO ALLEGEDLY PREFERRED ORAL SEX DURING *HIS* EXTRA-MARITAL ENCOUNTERS -- SO THAT HE COULD SAY *HE* HAD NOT HAD "SEX"...

DO AS--

...*DAN BURTON*... FAMOUS FOR CALLING THE PRESIDENT A "SCUMBAG," IT TURNS OUT THAT BURTON IS ACTUALLY THE FATHER OF AN OUT-OF-WEDLOCK *CHILD*...

--I SAY--

...*HELEN CHENOWETH*... ANOTHER OUTSPOKEN CLINTON CRITIC WHO, AS IT HAPPENS, HAS REPORTEDLY HAD NUMEROUS AFFAIRS--AND LIED ABOUT THEM...

--NOT AS--

...AND *HENRY HYDE*...WHOSE LONG-RUNNING AFFAIR WITH A WOMAN THIRTY YEARS AGO DESTROYED HER *MAR-RIAGE.*

--I DID.

ALL *WE* CAN FIGURE IS THAT THIS IS EITHER A *REALLY BAD DREAM* --OR THE ENTIRE NATION'S WATER SUPPLY HAS BEEN SPIKED WITH A POWERFUL, LONG-LASTING *HALLUCINOGEN.*

MONICA IS, LIKE, A METAPHOR FOR *LIFE*--YOU KNOW?

OH, MAN... THIS IS, LIKE, *TOO* INTENSE...

I HOPE IT *NEVER* WEARS OFF!

RUSH

(ORIGINALLY APPEARED ON THE COVER OF THE *VILLAGE VOICE.*)

25

THIS MODERN WORLD

by TOM TOMORROW

THINGS TOM TO-MORROW WORRIES ABOUT AT THREE IN THE MORNING...

WILL ANY-ONE READ MY STRIP--

--IF I GET TOO LONG-WINDED AND WONKY?

BIFF, THIS IS THE RICHEST COUNTRY IN THE WORLD AND YET 30 MILLION AMERICANS GO WITH-OUT *HEALTH INSURANCE!* THE *ONLY* LOGICAL SOLUTION IS A SINGLE PAYER SYSTEM WHICH WOULD COVER *EVERYONE* WHILE ACTUALLY *REDUCING COSTS* BY ELIMINATING THE PARASITICAL, FOR-PROFIT *INSURANCE INDUSTRY--*

AAK!

...IF MY POP CULTURE REFERENCES ARE JUST *TOO DAMN OBSCURE?*

OH NO! THAT GIANT HAS AS FIRM A GRIP ON VALERIE AS *CORPORATE LOBBYISTS* HAVE ON THE *AMERICAN POLITICAL SYSTEM!*

...IF I GET *TOO SELF-REFERENTIAL?*

WILL ANY-ONE READ MY STRIP--

WILL ANY-ONE READ MY STRIP--

WILL ANY-ONE READ MY STRIP--

WILL ANY-ONE READ MY STRIP--

WILL ANY-ONE READ MY ST--

...OR--WORST OF ALL-- IF I GO A WEEK WITHOUT MEN-MENTIONING *MONICA LEWINSKY?*

HEY--WHAT GIVES? THIS CARTOON DOESN'T CON-TAIN A *SINGLE* JOKE ABOUT THE PRESIDENT'S *SEX LIFE!*

BOY, HAS TOM TOMOR-ROW EVER LET US DOWN *THIS* WEEK!

26

THIS MODERN WORLD

by TOM TOMORROW

27

THIS MODERN WORLD

by TOM TOMORROW

Panel 1: MORE JOURNALISTIC MEA CULPAS: THE RELEASE OF GARY WEBB'S NEW BOOK, *DARK ALLIANCE*, PROMPTS *THE NEW YORK TIMES* TO APOLOGIZE FOR ITS CLUMSY ATTEMPTS TO DISCREDIT HIS WORK ON THE CONNECTIONS BETWEEN THE CONTRAS, CRACK DEALERS, AND THE *CIA*...

> WE IGNORED WEBB'S EXHAUSTIVE DOCUMENTATION-- WHILE REPORTING THAT THE CIA HAD EXONERATED *ITSELF*!

> IT'S A WONDER WE HAVE ANY CREDIBILITY LEFT AT *ALL*!

Panel 2: THE *WASHINGTON POST* IS SIMILARLY MOVED TO APOLOGIZE FOR *ITS* ATTACK ON WEBB, WRITTEN BY A MAN NAMED WALTER PINCUS-- WHO, THE POST FAILED TO DISCLOSE, ACTUALLY *WORKED FOR THE CIA* AS A YOUNG MAN...

> WE COMPLETELY VIOLATED THE TRUST OF OUR READERS -- AND MADE A *MOCKERY* OF JOURNALISTIC OBJECTIVITY!

> OUR ENTIRE EDITORIAL STAFF HAS DECIDED TO RESIGN IN *SHAME*!

Panel 3: MEANWHILE, THE *CINCINNATI ENQUIRER* APOLOGIZES PROFUSELY FOR RETRACTING THEIR ENTIRE SERIES OF ARTICLES ON *CHIQUITA'S* UNSAVORY BUSINESS PRACTICES, AFTER A REPORTER WAS FOUND TO HAVE ILLEGALLY ACCESSED CHIQUITA'S VOICEMAIL SYSTEM...

> --EVEN THOUGH MANY OF THE ARTICLES WERE BASED ON FIRSTHAND REPORTING AND HAD *NOTHING TO DO* WITH THE VOICEMAIL MESSAGES!

> LET'S FACE IT-- WE CAVED LIKE *MISERABLE, SPINELESS WORMS*!

Panel 4: FINALLY, *CNN* AND *TIME* ISSUE A *JOINT APOLOGY*--FOR SERVING AS UNCRITICAL PENTAGON MOUTHPIECES DURING THE *GULF WAR*, THAT IS...

> 'LIBERAL MEDIA' MY ASS! ALL WE *DID* DURING THAT WAR WAS PARROT ADMINISTRATION PROPAGANDA!

> THEY TOLD US TO JUMP-- AND WE ASKED HOW *HIGH*!

> WE ONLY HOPE YOU CAN FIND IT IN YOUR HEART TO *FORGIVE* US!

> HEY, A FELLA CAN *DREAM*...

tomorrow@well.com

TOM TOMORROW © 8-12-98

THIS MODERN WORLD

by TOM TOMORROW

IT'S TMW'S DIRECTOR OF MARKETING-- *BOB FRIENDLY!*

SPARKY, WE'RE *NEVER* GOING TO WIDEN OUR AUDIENCE IF WE DON'T GIVE EDITORS WHAT THEY WANT--SINGLE-PANEL CARTOONS WITH AS FEW WORDS AS *POSSIBLE!*

OKAY--LET'S GIVE IT A TRY!

UM-- REALLY?

SURE! AS LONG AS WE CAN COME UP WITH A SINGLE IMAGE WHICH ENCAPSULATES MY UTTER AMBIVALENCE TOWARD THE FATE OF A PRESIDENT WHO SUPPORTED NAFTA, GATT, AND WELFARE REFORM--*AND WHO* SCREWED UP OUR BEST SHOT AT HEALTH CARE REFORM IN *DECADES* BY GETTING INTO BED WITH *BIG INSURERS!*

ER--

I'D ALSO LIKE TO NOTE THAT CLINTON PROBABLY *IS* DIRTY AS HELL ON WHITEWATER, FILEGATE, AND SO ON--AND THAT THE STARR REPORT'S SINGLE-MINDED FOCUS ON PERJURY MAY WELL BE THE EQUIVALENT OF NAILING A MOBSTER ON *TAX EVASION* WHEN YOU JUST CAN'T FIND A SMOKING GUN ANYWHERE *ELSE!*

OF COURSE, WE'LL NEED TO POINT OUT THAT THE STRATEGY HAS BACKFIRED, LARGELY BECAUSE STARR IS A MORALISTIC *PRIG* WHO FAILED TO ANTICIPATE THAT THE PUBLIC WOULD BE ANYTHING LESS THAN *OUTRAGED*--WHICH ITSELF RAISES INTERESTING QUESTIONS VIS-A-VIS THE SUPPOSED *CONSERVATISM* OF AVERAGE AMERICANS...

AND JUST TO KEEP EVERYTHING IN PERSPECTIVE, IT'S ALSO WORTH NOTING THAT WHILE CLINTON'S ETHICS ARE CLEARLY SITUATIONAL, STARR IS SOMETHING OF A MORAL RELATIVIST AS WELL-- AT LEAST WHEN IT COMES TO ILLEGALLY-RECORDED *PHONE CONVERSATIONS* AND GRAND JURY *LEAKS!*

SO--WHADDYA *THINK?*

UH-MAYBE WE CAN TRY *NEXT* WEEK.

NO PROBLEM! I'M HOPING TO CONTRAST THE STRICT NEW *BANKRUPTCY LAWS* WITH THE BAILOUT OF THAT HUGE *HEDGE FUND* AND DISCUSS THE HYPOCRISY OF BLAH BLAH BLAH BLAH BLAH BLAH BLAH

SIGH...I WONDER IF "DILBERT" HAS ANY JOB OPENINGS THESE DAYS...

TOM TOMORROW ©10-14-98 ... www.thismodernworld.com

29

THIS MODERN WORLD

by TOM TOMORROW

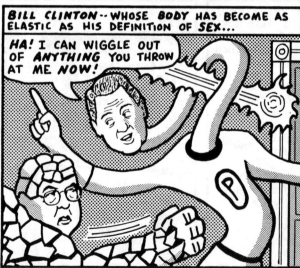

30

THIS MODERN WORLD

by TOM TOMORROW

CHRISTIAN CONSERVATIVES CLAIM THAT SEXUAL ORIENTATION IS A MATTER OF *CHOICE.*

MAN--THAT NEW AIDE IS *HUNKY!*

NO! MUSN'T THINK ABOUT IT! I HAVE *CHOSEN* TO BE *HETEROSEXUAL!*

TRENT

THEY SEEM TO BELIEVE THAT ANY VARIATION FROM THE NORM THREATENS SOCIETY AS A *WHOLE--*

WHO DO THESE *LEFT-HANDED* PEOPLE THINK THEY *ARE,* ANYWAY? THEY SHOULD USE THEIR *RIGHT* HANDS--LIKE *NORMAL* AMERICANS!

WE'VE GOT TO *WARN* EVERY-ONE ABOUT THE INSIDIOUS *SOUTHPAW AGENDA!*

--AND THAT AMERICA IS A NATION IN SPIRITUAL DECLINE--IN NEED OF RELIGIOUS GUIDANCE ONLY *THEY* CAN PROVIDE--

PREFERABLY ENSHRINED IN *LAW!* IT'S TIME TO PUT *GOD* BACK IN *GOVERNMENT!*

IF IT WORKED FOR THE *TALI-BAN,* IT CAN WORK FOR *US!*

--TO WHICH WE CAN ONLY SAY: TELL IT TO *MATTHEW SHEPARD'S* FAMILY.

OH, COME ON! WHAT *POSSIBLE* CONNECTION COULD THERE BE BE-TWEEN HOMOPHOBIC *RHETORIC--*

--AND HOMOPHOBIC *VIOLENCE?*

I THINK *TOM TOMORROW* IS THE *REAL* BIGOT HERE!

HE IS INTOLER-ANT...OF OUR *INTOLERANCE!*

TOM TOMORROW © 10-28-98

THIS MODERN WORLD
by TOM TOMORROW

ACCORDING TO A REPORT FROM HERITAGE FOUNDATION ANALYST ROBERT RECTOR, POVERTY IN AMERICA IS *VASTLY OVERSTATED*...BECAUSE, AMONG OTHER THINGS--

--MANY OF THE SO-CALLED *POOR* ACTUALLY OWN *VCR'S*--AND *COLOR TELEVISIONS!*

WOW! *COLOR* TEE-VEES? THEY MUST BE *ROLLIN'* IN THE DOUGH!

NOW, AS COMPELLING AS HIS LOGIC MAY BE, MR. RECTOR *DOES* SEEM TO BE OVERLOOKING THAT SMALL FACT OF MODERN LIFE KNOWN AS THE *CREDIT CARD INDUSTRY*...

HELLO! AM I SPEAKING TO A *CARBON-BASED LIFE FORM?*

UM--I GUESS SO...

GREAT! THAT MEANS *YOU'RE* ELIGIBLE FOR A $5000 LINE OF CREDIT FROM *VISA INTERNATIONAL!*

...WHICH NOT ONLY ALLOWS THE POOR TO *OWN* SUCH EXTRAVAGANT LUXURIES AS, UM, COLOR TEEVEES--BUT TO SPEND THE NEXT FORTY YEARS *PAYING* FOR THEM AS WELL...

AND WITH THE NEW BANK-RUPTCY LAWS, YOU'D BETTER BELIEVE THEY'RE *GONNA* PAY! FINANCIAL IRRESPONSIBILITY WILL NO LONGER BE REWARDED IN *THIS* SOCIETY!

UNLESS YOU HAPPEN TO RUN A HIGH RISK *HEDGE FUND*, OF COURSE.

THE REST OF THE REPORT'S FINDINGS HAVE AN EQUALLY TANGENTIAL RELATIONSHIP TO REALITY-- AND WILL UNDOUBTEDLY GROW EVEN *MORE* DISTORTED AS THEY ARE PASSED ALONG THE INTERNET AND TALK RADIO...

I HEARD THAT THE POOR EAT AT FOUR STAR RESTAURANTS EVERY NIGHT--AT TAXPAYER EXPENSE!

I HEARD THEY ALL HAVE SWIMMING POOLS FILLED WITH *CHAMPAGNE* --PAID FOR BY THE GOVERNMENT!

NOT TO MENTION *COLOR* TEEVEES!

MAN, THEY MUST BE LIVIN' THE GOOD LIFE!

THIS MODERN WORLD

by TOM TOMORROW

POLITICIANS INVOKE THEM AT EVERY OPPORTUNITY.

THE AMERICAN PEOPLE SENT ME HERE TO DO A JOB! AND I WON'T BE DISTRACTED FROM THE WORK OF THE AMERICAN PEOPLE! BECAUSE THAT IS WHAT THE AMERICAN PEOPLE WANT!

PUNDITS ARGUE ABOUT THEM *INCESSANTLY.*

BILL, *THE AMERICAN PEOPLE* THINK YOU'RE AN IGNORANT WIENERHEAD!

DO *NOT!*

DO *TOO!*

NUH UH!

UH HUH!

N.P.R. CORRESPONDENTS OCCASIONALLY VENTURE OUT INTO THE HEARTLAND IN *SEARCH* OF THEM.

POLITICIANS ARE OUT OF *TOUCH!* THEY OUGHTA COME HELP ME SLOP TH' HOGS SOMETIME!

THEN THEY'D KNOW A THING OR TWO ABOUT *HOG SLOPPIN',* AT LEAST!

THERE YOU HAVE IT! SIMPLE HOMESPUN WISDOM STRAIGHT FROM THE MOUTH OF *THE AMERICAN PEOPLE!* BACK TO YOU, NOAH!

OF COURSE, WHEN ELECTION DAY ROLLS AROUND, THEY ARE USUALLY NOTABLE FOR THEIR *ABSENCE...*

THE AMERICAN PEOPLE HAVE SPOKEN! SENATOR TWEEDLEDUM HAS DEFEATED CANDIDATE TWEEDLEDEE BY ONE VOTE -- THE *ONLY VOTE CAST!*

I WAS REALLY JUST LOOKING FOR THE BATHROOM -- BUT I FIGURED, HECK! I'M HERE! WHY *NOT* VOTE?

SO -- WHO IS THIS TWEEDLEDUM GUY, ANYWAY?

ACTION McNEWS

ACTION McNEWS

AC McI

...AND THEN IT'S BACK TO BUSINESS AS USUAL... ALL IN THE NAME OF *YOU KNOW WHO...*

SENATOR, WE AT *TOXIC SLUDGECO* SUPPORT THE VALUABLE WORK YOU'RE DOING FOR THE *THE AMERICAN PEOPLE!*

THAT'S MIGHTY KIND OF YOU! I THINK *THE AMERICAN PEOPLE* MIGHT JUST BE CRYING OUT FOR A *LARGE CORPORATE TAX CUT* THIS YEAR!

YES, I *THOUGHT* THEY MIGHT BE...

WINK! WINK!

WINK!

THIS MODERN WORLD

by TOM TOMORROW

SO I'M AWAY ON A BOOK TOUR FOR A COUPLE OF WEEKS--AND THE POLITICAL LANDSCAPE *EXPLODES.*

GRATUITOUS PLUG FOR NEW BOOK

PENGUIN SOUP FOR THE SOUL

BY TOM TOMORROW

THE GOOD CITIZENS OF MINNESOTA ELECT A PRO-FESSIONAL *WRESTLER* FOR GOVERNOR.

NEWT GINGRICH ENDS UP LOSING *HIS* JOB BECAUSE THE PRESIDENT BONKED AN INTERN.

AND JUST TO KEEP THINGS INTERESTING, THE ADMINI-STRATION ALMOST STARTS DROPPING BOMBS ON *IRAQ* AGAIN.*

*AND MAYBE HAS, BY THE TIME YOU READ THIS.

I SUPPOSE WHEN I LEAVE FOR *CHRISTMAS,* THE MILI-TARY WILL ANNEX *CANADA* ...OR MAYBE *AL GORE* WILL HAVE A *SEX CHANGE OPERATION...*

HONESTLY-- I CAN'T LEAVE YOU KIDS ALONE FOR A *MINUTE!!*

TOM TOMORROW © 12-2-98 • www.thismodernworld.com

THIS MODERN WORLD

by TOM TOMORROW

AT THIS POINT, BILL CLINTON MUST BE FEELING PRETTY MUCH IMPEACHMENT-PROOF.

I'VE SPENT MILLIONS OF TAXPAYER DOLLARS ON *SLEAZY SEX* WITH *PRE-OP TRANSSEXUAL PROSTITUTES!* AND I SHOT *VINCE FOSTER* JUST TO WATCH HIM *DIE!*

IT'S ALL ON *VIDEOTAPE!* AND HERE'S A *SIGNED CONFESSION!*

COME AND *GET ME,* SUCKERS!

THE ENTIRE PROCESS HAS OBVIOUSLY LOST MOMENTUM--AND WASN'T EXACTLY REVITALIZED BY *KEN STARR'S* TESTIMONY...

OH, WHAT LIBERAL *HOGWASH!* HIS RUMINATIONS ON THE MEANING OF RULE 6(e) WERE NOTHING SHORT OF *SPELLBINDING!*

I THINK HE'S JUST *DREAMY!* I WISH THAT SOMEDAY HE'D SMILE THAT STRANGE LITTLE SMILE AT ME!

BASICALLY, CLINTON IS THE *INDIANA JONES* OF AMERICAN POLITICS... THRILLING AUDIENCES WITH ONE NARROW ESCAPE AFTER *ANOTHER--*

UH OH...

--WHILE HIS ENEMIES DEFEAT *THEMSELVES.*

BILL--HE'S GOING TO *OPEN IT--*

CLOSE YOUR EYES, HILLARY! DON'T PAY *ANY ATTENTION!*

HEY--WHAT-- NO! IT'S HIM YOU WANT! NOT ME! NOT MEEEE-

NEWT

STARR REPORT

TOM TOMORROW ©12-16-98

35

THIS MODERN WORLD

by TOM TOMORROW

SINCE THE ELECTION OF JESSE VENTURA, MINNESO-TANS HAVE BEEN SUBJECTED TO A BARRAGE OF ONE-LINERS AND CHEAP GAGS MASQUERADING AS POLITICAL COMMENTARY.

SO TO HELP PROMOTE A MORE *INFORMED* PUBLIC DISCOURSE, *WE'VE* DECIDED TO PRESENT THE FOLLOW-ING *BACKGROUNDER* ON "THE NORTH STAR STATE!"

--A NICKNAME DERIVED FROM THE STATE'S POETIC AND EVOCATIVE MOTTO-- "*L'ÉTOILE DU NORD!*"

THE STATE BIRD IS THE *COMMON LOON*--ONE OF THE EARTH'S *OLD-EST BIRD SPECIES!* THE STATE *TREE* IS THE TOWERING *NOR-WAY PINE*--AND THE STATE *FLOWER* IS THE LOVELY *PINK AND WHITE LADY-SLIPPER!*

AND OF COURSE, MIN-NESOTANS HAVE CHOS-EN TO CELEBRATE RE-FRESHING, WHOLESOME *MILK* AS THEIR STATE *DRINK*--WHILE PROUDLY PROCLAIMING THE TASTY *BLUE-BERRY MUFFIN* TO BE THEIR OFFICIAL STATE *MUFFIN!**

* THIS IS ALL TRUE, INCIDENTALLY.

THE STATE SEAL OF MINNE-SOTA FEATURES A PLOWMAN, SYMBOLIZING PIONEER AGRI-CULTURE--AND A NATIVE AMERICAN RIDING TOWARD A SETTING SUN, REPRESENTING "THE WHITE MAN REPLACING THE INDIAN IN MINNESOTA!"*

INTERESTINGLY, MINNESOTA HAS MORE THAN 11,000 LAKES--A GREATER WATER AREA THAN *ANY OTHER STATE!*

* ACCORDING TO THE 1959 EDITION OF THE WORLD BOOK ENCYCLOPEDIA.

WELL, THAT'S ALL WE HAVE ROOM FOR THIS WEEK --BUT WE HOPE THAT THE NEXT TIME SOME JOKESTER STARTS "CRACKING WISE" ABOUT OUR 32ND STATE, *YOU'LL* HAVE JUST A *LITTLE MORE PERSPECTIVE* ON THE ISSUE...

SURE, DAVID LETTER-MAN CAN MAKE HIS LITTLE "JOKES"--BUT IS *HE* AWARE THAT MINNESOTA IS ALSO KNOWN AS "THE GOPHER STATE"--

--DUE TO A PRE-PONDERANCE OF *STRIPED GROUND SQUIRRELS?*

PROBABLY *NOT*-- BUT NOW *YOU* ARE!

TOM TOMORROW © 12-9-98 • www.thismodernworld.com

36

THIS MODERN WORLD

by TOM TOMORROW

Panel 1: A FEW WEEKS AGO, WE CASUALLY NOTED THAT THE IMPEACHMENT PROCESS HAD "OBVIOUSLY LOST MOMENTUM."

THIS WAS A TERRIBLE MISTAKE -- AND WE *APOLOGIZE!* WE ARE *VERY SORRY* FOR MISLEADING THE AMERICAN PEOPLE -- AND WE *DEEPLY REGRET* THE PAIN AND EMBARRASSMENT WE MAY HAVE CAUSED OUR *EDITORS* --

OH, SHUT THE HELL UP.

Panel 2: IN REALITY, OF COURSE, THE REPUBLICANS CHARGED FULL STEAM AHEAD WITH THEIR LITTLE SHOW TRIAL...

THE PRESIDENT TOLD A *LIE!* THIS IS TRULY THE MOST SHOCKING EVENT IN THE HISTORY OF OUR NATION!

HE *MUST* BE IMPEACHED -- LEST OUR SOCIETY COLLAPSE INTO LAWLESS, BLOOD-DRENCHED *AN-ARCHY!*

Panel 3: ...WHILE THE DEMOCRATS REITERATED *THEIR* MESSAGE AS RELENTLESSLY AS DISNEY AUDIO-ANIMATRONS.

WHAT THE PRESIDENT DID WAS *WRONG* -- BUT IT DOES *NOT* RISE TO THE LEVEL OF AN IMPEACHABLE OFFENSE -- *CLICK!*

-- AN IMPEACHABLE OFFENSE -- *CLICK!* -- AN IMPEACHABLE OFFENSE -- *CLICK!*

COULD SOMEONE HAND ME A SCREW-DRIVER?

Panel 4: AND WHILE WE'RE A LITTLE LEERY OF MAKING ANY MORE BLANKET ASSERTIONS AT THIS POINT, ONE THING SEEMS CERTAIN: THE BULLSHIT IS GONNA GET A *LOT DEEP-ER* BEFORE THIS IS ALL OVER...

I'M WORRIED ABOUT ALL THE CHIL-DREN WHO LOOK TO THE PRESIDENT FOR *MORAL GUIDANCE!*

BIFF, WHO WAS PRESIDENT WHEN YOU WERE A BOY?

RICHARD NIXON, OF COURSE! WHY?

OH -- NEVER MIND...

TOM TOMORROW ©98

THIS MODERN WORLD

by TOM TOMORROW

Panel 1:

ISN'T IT A LITTLE ODD HOW EVERY CHRISTMAS SEASON, THERE'S *ONE HOT TOY* PARENTS SUDDENLY *HAVE* TO FIND FOR THEIR CHILDREN?

OH MY GOD! IS THAT A GENUINE *RANT-AND-RAVE SPARKY* DOLL?

IT SURE IS! WHEN YOU PUSH HIS TUMMY, HE DECRIES THE INFLUENCE OF CORPORATE MONEY ON THE AMERICAN POLITICAL SYSTEM!

OUR KID IS GONNA *LOVE* IT!

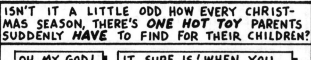

Panel 2:

MAYBE THE WHOLE THING IS A *SCAM*...MAYBE SOME P.R. FIRM HIRES ACTORS TO GO INTO STORES AND STIR UP A FUSS ABOUT THE TOY IN QUESTION...

I'M BUYING *ALL* THE RANT-AND-RAVE SPARKYS IN THIS STORE BECAUSE THEY ARE *SO POPULAR* AND *HARD TO FIND!*

CURSE YOU! WHATEVER WILL *MY* CHILDREN DO WITHOUT THEIR VERY *OWN* RANT-AND-RAVE SPARKY DOLLS?

REDUCED!

SALE!

BARBIE

Panel 3:

...LEADING TV NEWS DEPARTMENTS -- WHO ARE, OF COURSE, ALWAYS HUNGRY FOR HOLIDAY NEWS FILLER -- TO *COVER* THE STORY...

BETTY, IT LOOKS LIKE THE RANT-AND-RAVE SPARKY IS THE MOST DESIRABLE TOY IN *HUMAN HISTORY!* PARENTS ARE CLAWING EACH OTHERS' *EYES* OUT FOR THE CHANCE TO PURCHASE ONE!

WELL, BIFF, IT'S CLEAR THAT ANYONE LUCKY ENOUGH TO *FIND* A RANT-AND-RAVE SPARKY DOLL SHOULD BUY IT *RIGHT AWAY* -- WHETHER THEY HAVE CHILDREN OR *NOT!*

TOYS-Я-WE

ACTION McNEW

ACTION McNEW

Panel 4:

...CREATING A VERITABLE *FRENZY* -- AT LEAST UNTIL *CHRISTMAS MORNING*...

ISN'T IT *WONDERFUL*, SON?

YOU'LL BE THE ENVY OF *ALL* YOUR FRIENDS!

UM...THANKS... I GUESS...

WHAT IS IT -- A TALKING *DUCK?*

-- OF COURSE THESE BOUGHT-AND-PAID-FOR *POLITICIANS* WILL *NEVER* ENACT SUBSTANTIVE REFORM --

TOM TOMORROW ©12-23-98

THIS MODERN WORLD

by TOM TOMORROW

THIS MODERN WORLD

by TOM TOMORROW

NOTES FROM A STRANGE POLITICAL SEASON... CLINTON'S BOMBING OF IRAQ COINCIDES EXACTLY WITH THE HOUSE IMPEACHMENT VOTE--BUT ANYONE WHO QUESTIONS HIS TIMING IS DERIDED AS A *CYNIC*...

HMM...SO WHAT DO YOU CALL SOMEONE WHO UNQUESTIONINGLY *ACCEPTS* THE EXPLANATIONS OF A KNOWN LIAR WITH A PENCHANT FOR RECKLESS BEHAVIOR AND A GROWING HISTORY OF SUSPICIOUSLY-TIMED MILITARY ACTIONS?

WHY--A *GOOD DEMOCRAT*, OF COURSE!

BOB LIVINGSTON RESIGNS AS *HIS* ADULTEROUS PAST IS MADE PUBLIC...AND AN APPARENTLY UNDISTINGUISHED BACK-BENCHER IS SELECTED AS THE *NEW* SPEAKER OF THE HOUSE...

AFTER AN EXHAUSTIVE SEARCH WE HAVE DETERMINED THAT DENNIS HASTERT--

--IS THE ONLY REPUBLICAN WE CAN FIND WHO'S *NEVER HAD AN AFFAIR!*

BY GOD, HE'S GOT *MY* VOTE!

WE MAY BE TALKING *PRESIDENTIAL* MATERIAL HERE, BOYS!

A PECULIAR ASSORTMENT OF PRESIDENTIAL DEFENDERS CONTINUE TO HACK THEIR WAY THROUGH A SEMANTIC *THICKET*...DECRYING THE DISPROPORTIONATE RESPONSE OF IMPEACHMENT, THE REV. AL SHARPTON DECLARES THAT "YOU DON'T USE A *SLEDGEHAMMER* TO SMASH A *COCKROACH*..."

UH--MAYBE WE COULD ALL PUT A LITTLE MORE WORK INTO THOSE *METAPHORS*..?

AND FINALLY... *LINDA TRIPP* IS SAID TO HAVE A TEAM OF ADVISORS WORKING ON AN IMAGE MAKEOVER...AND WE CAN'T *WAIT* TO SEE HOW *THAT* ONE WORKS OUT...

I DIDN'T REALIZE SHE WAS TRYING TO *HELP* MONICA BY SURREPTITIOUSLY TAPING THEIR CONVERSATIONS!

IT MAKES SENSE-- NOW THAT WE KNOW ABOUT HER LIFETIME OF SACRIFICE AND DEVOTION TO THE NEEDS OF *OTHERS!*

WHEN I GROW UP I WANT TO BE *JUST LIKE HER!*

40

THIS MODERN WORLD

by TOM TOMORROW

1999 A LOOK BACK

AH, TO RE-LIVE THE YOUTHFUL EXUBERANCE OF THOSE GLORIOUS, CAREFREE DAYS!

HEY--REMEMBER HOW THE *MONICA VIRUS* INFECTED OUR BRAINS THAT YEAR?

THE FIRST VICTIMS WERE TV NEWSCASTERS...OF COURSE, NO ONE REALLY NOTICED ANYTHING DIFFERENT AT FIRST...

OUR TOP STORY TO-NIGHT--A FIVE CAR PILEUP ON INTER-STATE 80!

SOURCES SAY THE CRASH HAD NOTHING TO DO WITH THE PRESIDENT'S SEX LIFE! FOR MORE ON THE STORY, LET'S GO LIVE TO THE *WHITE HOUSE!*

ACTION McNEWS

ACTION McNEWS

ACT McN

...BUT SLOWLY, WE BEGAN TO REALIZE THAT THE PRESIDENTIAL SEX SCANDAL HAD BECOME *INESCAPABLE* -- NO MATTER *WHERE* WE TURNED...

"Daddy says cigars are okay -- as long as you don't inhale!"

...AND THAT NONE OF US WERE CAPABLE OF COMPLETING A *SENTENCE* WITHOUT MENTIONING IT SOMEHOW...

I'M HOME, DEAR! WHAT THE PRESIDENT DID WAS CLEARLY WRONG -- BUT IT DIDN'T RISE TO THE LEVEL OF IM-PEACHMENT!

YES, BUT WHAT KIND OF EXAMPLE DOES THIS SET FOR THE *CHILDREN*? AND HOW WAS YOUR DAY?

SCIENTISTS THEORIZED THAT OUR ENTIRE SOCIETY WAS SUFFERING FROM *SCANDAL OVERLOAD SYNDROME*... BUT BY THAT POINT, THEY WERE IN NO CONDITION TO DO ANYTHING *ABOUT* IT...

MUST CONCENTRATE... MUST FIND A CURE... IT WASN'T ABOUT SEX-- IT WAS ABOUT THE *LIES!*

MAYBE IF WE JOLTED THE SYNAPSES... WITH ELECTRICITY...BUT WE *ALL* LIE ABOUT SEX!

$x^2 \cdot 3 \sqrt{12}$

$C = MoNiCA$?

THEN, OF COURSE, THE Y2K GLITCH CAUSED OUR COMPUTERS TO GO HAYWIRE AND WE WERE ALL ENSLAVED BY KILLER ROBOTS.

WE SURE DIDN'T SEE *THAT* ONE COMING! OH WELL-AT LEAST IT TOOK OUR MINDS OFF YOU-KNOW-WHO...

CEASE YOUR CHATTER, BIO-LOGICAL UNITS --OR BE *DESTROYED!*

THIS MODERN WORLD

by TOM TOMORROW

--AND MY GUEST THIS WEEK ON *DRUDGE* IS, AS USUAL, *LUCIANNE GOLDBERG*! LUCIANNE, LET'S TALK ABOUT *ME* SOME MORE! I WAS THE ONE WHO *BROKE* THE LEWINSKY STORY, YOU KNOW!

YOU SURE WERE, MATT! *COUGH! COUGH!*

I'VE INFLUENCED THE COURSE OF AMERICAN POLITICS! I'M A HOUSEHOLD NAME! LOOK AT THIS-- I'VE EVEN GOT MY OWN *TV SHOW!*

YOU SURE DO, MATT! *COUGH!*

OF COURSE, I LIKE TO BALANCE TALK OF MY IMPRESSIVE AND WELL-DESERVED SUCCESS WITH AN AIR OF *MOCK HUMILITY!* AFTER ALL--

--WHO WOULD HAVE *EVER* FIGURED THAT A GOOFY LOOKING GUY WITH A NAME LIKE *"DRUDGE"*--

--WHO LIVES IN A SHABBY APARTMENT IN WEST HOLLYWOOD! DON'T FORGET THAT PART! *COUGH! HAK!*

--WOULD BREAK THE *SINGLE MOST IMPORTANT STORY IN HUMAN HISTORY*?! HUH? WHO WOULDA FIGURED, LUCIANNE? HUH? WHO WOULDA *FIGURED*?

ONLY THE PEOPLE WHO SPOON FED YOU THE STORY, HON...

WHAT'S THAT, LUCIANNE?

UH-- NOTHING! *HAK! COUGH! HAK!*

TUNE IN NEXT WEEK FOR *MORE* INSIGHTS -- FROM THE GUY WHO BROKE A STORY ONCE!

TOM TOMORROW ©1999 · 2-10-99

THIS MODERN WORLD
by TOM TOMORROW

Panel 1:

YOU CAN READ THE DAILY PAPER AND WATCH THE CABLE NEWS CHANNELS AND TRUST THE RESPONSIBLE VOICES OF AUTHORITY TO TELL YOU WHAT YOU NEED TO KNOW -- ABOUT IRAQ, SAY...

IF SADDAM WAS GOING TO KEEP TREATING THE U.N. INSPECTORS LIKE *SPIES*-

--WE HAD NO *CHOICE* BUT TO BOMB HIM!

THAT MADMAN HAS *NO RESPECT* FOR THE INTERNATIONAL RULE OF LAW!

Panel 2:

...AND WHEN IT TURNS OUT THAT THERE WAS MORE TO THE STORY THAN YOU WERE TOLD, YOU CAN TREAT IT AS SOME SORT OF *FREAKISH ABERRATION*...

WHADDYA KNOW! THE UNSCOM TEAM REALLY *WAS* SPYING FOR THE U.S.!

SO OUR GOVERNMENT SUBVERTED U.N. AUTONOMY AND ESSENTIALLY *MANUFACTURED* AN EXCUSE TO BOMB IRAQ?

OH WELL! I'M SURE IT WILL NEVER HAPPEN AGAIN!

Panel 3:

...BUT THE THING IS, THERE'S *ALWAYS* MORE TO THE STORY...FOR INSTANCE, YOU CAN WATCH THE RESPONSIBLE AND SOBER VOICES OF AUTHORITY REHASH THE *IMPEACHMENT* DEBATE UNTIL YOUR *EYES BLEED*--

BLAH BLAH BLAH HIGH CRIMES AND MISDEMEANORS BLAH BLA CONSTITUTIONAL DUTY

I'M...SO...WELL... INFORMED...

BLAH BLAH TIME TO MOVE ON BLAH BLAH THE AMER PEOPLE BLAH

Panel 4:

--BUT THERE'S *STILL* GONNA BE MORE GOING ON THAN YOU'LL PROBABLY EVER *KNOW*...

YOU GUYS WRAP THIS UP QUICKLY AND NOBODY SEES THE PHOTOS OF ORRIN HATCH WITH THE *FARM ANIMALS*!

DON'T FORGET ABOUT MY TAPES OF HILLARY HAVING PHONE SEX WITH *MADELEINE ALBRIGHT*, PAL!

LOOK, WE DO THIS *MY WAY*-- OR *EVERYBODY* FINDS OUT ABOUT THAT THREESOME BETWEEN THE TWO OF YOU--AND LINDA *TRIPP*!

TOM TOMORROW 2-3-99

43

THIS MODERN WORLD

by TOM TOMORROW

Panel 1: I DON'T KNOW WHAT'S GOING TO BE HAPPENING WITH THE IMPEACHMENT TRIAL BY THE TIME YOU READ THIS CARTOON...

--THOUGH IT WOULD CERTAINLY BE AMUSING TO POSTULATE AN UNLIKELY SCENARIO OF WHAT *MIGHT* HAPPEN--AND THEN CARRY THAT SCENARIO THROUGH TO AN *ABSURD CONCLUSION!*

I'M QUAKING WITH MIRTH JUST *THINKING* ABOUT IT!

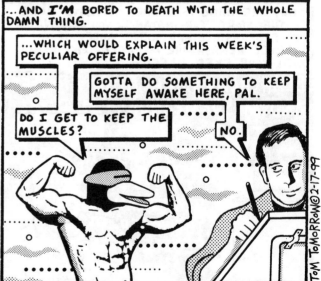

Panel 2: ...BUT I KNOW THIS MUCH: CLINTON IS AN OPPORTUNISTIC *SLIMEBALL*...

IN FACT, ONE OF THE MOST PUZZLING ASPECTS OF THIS ENTIRE SCANDAL HAS BEEN THE VEHEMENCE WITH WHICH LIBERALS CONTINUE TO *DEFEND* THE PRESIDENT--

--EVEN THOUGH HE'S DEMONSTRATED TIME AFTER TIME THAT HE'LL SELL THEM OUT IN A *HEARTBEAT* IF IT IS SOMEHOW TO HIS *ADVANTAGE!*

Panel 3: ...THE REPUBLICANS ARE *BLATANT* HYPOCRITES...

FOR INSTANCE, HYDE EXTOLS THE RULE OF LAW *TODAY*-- BUT DURING *IRAN-CONTRA*, HE DECLARED THAT "SOMETIMES YOU HAVE TO GO *ABOVE* THE WRITTEN LAW!"

AND AT THIS POINT, ONE HARDLY NEEDS TO RECOUNT THE LIST OF MORALISTIC REPUBLICANS-- INCLUDING HYDE -- WHO TURN OUT TO HAVE HAD ADULTEROUS AFFAIRS *THEMSELVES!*

Panel 4: ...AND *I'M* BORED TO DEATH WITH THE WHOLE DAMN THING.

...WHICH WOULD EXPLAIN THIS WEEK'S PECULIAR OFFERING.

GOTTA DO SOMETHING TO KEEP MYSELF AWAKE HERE, PAL.

DO I GET TO KEEP THE MUSCLES?

NO.

TOM TOMORROW ©2-17-99

44

THIS MODERN WORLD

by TOM TOMORROW

THESE DAYS, INVESTORS CAN'T THROW *ENOUGH* MONEY AT THE *INTERNET!*

YOU SEE, I'M WORKING ON A WEB SITE ABOUT MY *CAT!*

WHAT A *VISIONARY!*

SON, IF THERE AREN'T ENOUGH ZEROES ON THIS CHECK-- JUST *ADD SOME MORE!*

AMERICA ONLINE IS NOW WORTH ALMOST THREE TIMES AS MUCH AS *CBS*--WHILE AMAZON.COM, WHICH HAS YET TO SHOW A PROFIT, IS WORTH *ELEVEN* TIMES MORE THAN *BARNES & NOBLE!*

SAY, BIFF-- HAVE YOU EVER HEARD OF *TULIP MANIA..?*

WHAT'S THAT--A HOT NEW *INTERNET STARTUP?* HAVE THEY GONE *PUBLIC* YET? YOU CAN MAKE A *FORTUNE* IF YOU GET IN ON THE GROUND FLOOR, YOU KNOW!

NO *WONDER* THERE'S SUCH A RUSH TO TURN SOCIAL SECURITY OVER TO THESE *FINANCIAL GENIUSES!* SURE, THERE'S A BIT OF PARTISAN SQUABBLING OVER THE BEST WAY TO *DO* IT...

I THINK WE SHOULD INSTITUTE THIS FANTASTICALLY ILL-CONCEIVED NOTION WITH A *MODICUM* OF GOVERNMENTAL OVERSIGHT!

NONSENSE! WE SHOULD HAND THE FUTURE OF OUR NATION'S POOR AND ELDERLY TO WALL STREET INVESTMENT FIRMS WITH *NO STRINGS ATTACHED!*

LOTT

...BUT *DON'T WORRY!* ONE WAY OR ANOTHER, SOCIAL SECURITY'S GOING TO BE PRIVATIZED-- AND *THAT'S* GREAT NEWS FOR *EVERYONE*... ISN'T IT?

AH, MRS. MUGGLEWORTH, THE MARKET'S BEEN IN A BIT OF A SLUMP SINCE ALL THOSE *TECH STOCKS* TOOK A DIVE...

...BUT I'M *SURE* THINGS WILL PICK UP IN TEN OR FIFTEEN YEARS!

YOU'VE JUST GOT TO THINK *LONG TERM!*

SOCIAL SECURITY INC.

HELPING OURSELVES SINCE 1999

THIS MODERN WORLD

by TOM TOMORROW

BOY, I CAN'T TELL YOU HOW RELIEVED I AM THAT THE IMPEACHMENT TRIAL FIZZLED OUT! THOSE REPUBLICANS SURE HAVE EGG ON *THEIR* FACES, EH SPARKY?

UM...WALTER...

LOOK, THE DEFEAT OF HYPOCRITICAL BOZOS LIKE HENRY HYDE AND BOB BARR IS ADMITTEDLY GRATIFYING... BUT FOR GOD'S SAKE, MAN--DON'T BE SIMPLEMINDED! THIS WASN'T "US" VERSUS "THEM"! BILL CLINTON IS *NOT ON YOUR SIDE!*

CLINTON IS THE GUY WHO SIGNED *WELFARE REFORM* INTO LAW--WHO EAGERLY EMBRACED THE BLATANTLY HOMOPHOBIC *DEFENSE OF MARRIAGE ACT*--AND WHO'S DONE MORE DAMAGE TO CIVIL LIBERTIES THAN ANY PRESIDENT SINCE *RICHARD NIXON!*

HE'S ALSO THE GUY WHO BOMBED SUDAN, AFGHANISTAN AND IRAQ ON THE *FLIMSIEST* OF EXCUSES--BECAUSE IT WAS *POLITICALLY EXPEDIENT* TO DO SO! HELL, IF JUANITA BROADDRICK HAD ANY PHYSICAL EVIDENCE, WE'D PROBABLY BE AT WAR WITH *CANADA* BY NOW!

YES--BUT HE IS NOT A *REPUBLICAN!*

:SIGH:... I REALLY DON'T KNOW WHY I BOTHER...

TOM TOMORROW ©3-24-99

46

THIS MODERN WORLD

by TOM TOMORROW

SURE, EVERYONE *TRIES* TO APPEAR RATIONAL AND RESPONSIBLE...

I VISIT MY DENTIST AT *LEAST* TWICE A YEAR!

I FILL OUT THE WARRANTY CARD PROMPTLY AFTER *ANY* MAJOR PURCHASE!

I ROTATE MY TIRES EVERY SIX MONTHS-- JUST TO BE *SAFE!*

...BUT LET'S FACE IT--ONCE YOU SCRATCH THE SURFACE, MOST PEOPLE ARE PRETTY MUCH *NUTS...*

IF I KEEP PLAYING MY LUCKY NUMBERS I *KNOW* I'LL WIN THE LOTTERY *SOMEDAY!*

WHY WON'T THEY TELL US THE TRUTH ABOUT ROSWELL? WHAT ARE THEY *AFRAID* OF?

GOD HATES FAGS--I'M *SURE* HE DOES.

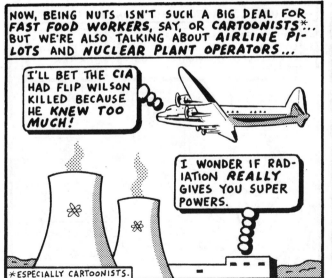

NOW, BEING NUTS ISN'T SUCH A BIG DEAL FOR *FAST FOOD WORKERS,* SAY, OR *CARTOONISTS*... BUT WE'RE ALSO TALKING ABOUT *AIRLINE PILOTS* AND *NUCLEAR PLANT OPERATORS...*

I'LL BET THE *CIA* HAD FLIP WILSON KILLED BECAUSE HE *KNEW TOO MUCH!*

I WONDER IF RADIATION *REALLY* GIVES YOU SUPER POWERS.

*ESPECIALLY CARTOONISTS.

...NOT TO MENTION *LEADERS OF THE FREE WORLD...*

--AND THEN I'D LICK WHIPPED CREAM OFF YASMINE BLEETH'S TAUT BREASTS WHILE CARMEN ELECTRA SWUNG FROM THE *TRAPEZE* WEARING NOTHING BUT A SKIMPY--

SIR! THE TROOPS ARE STANDING BY! SHALL WE COMMENCE THE *BOMBING?*

WHA--? OH-- YEAH, SURE... WHATEVER...

TOM TOMORROW© 3-17-99

THIS MODERN WORLD

by TOM TOMORROW

A BRIEF GUIDE TO THE NEW ECONOMY: A ROARING STOCK MARKET ENRICHES THE TOP TEN PERCENT OF AMERICANS--

--AND WHEN CONGLOMERATED MANUFACTURING ELIMINATED 1,500 JOBS, MY STOCK *DOUBLED!*

MAN! THE CASH JUST *GROWS ON TREES* THESE DAYS!

GRRR...

WILL WORK FOR CRUMBS

--INCLUDING MANY *PROFESSIONAL JOURNALISTS*-- WHO PRODUCE AN ENDLESS SUCCESSION OF UPBEAT ECONOMIC NEWS STORIES--

--AND WITH THE DOW AT RECORD LEVELS, IT SEEMS LIKE *EVERYONE* IS SHARING IN THE BOUNTY!

REPORTING LIVE FROM MY BRAND NEW S.U.V.-- I'M BIFF CHUCKLEHEAD!

BIFF1

--WHICH ARE DISSEMINATED TO THE VAST MAJORITY OF CITIZENS WHOSE REAL WAGES HAVE BEEN STAGNANT OR IN DECLINE SINCE THE *1970's*--

COMING UP NEXT-- A LOOK AT THE FABULOUS WORLD OF *CONSPICUOUS CONSUMPTION!*

YOU WANT FRIES WITH THAT?

DO I *LOOK* LIKE I'M MADE OF MONEY?

Diet Crap

--*ET VOILA!*-- A BOOMING ECONOMY IS CREATED!

HOW FORTUNATE WE ARE TO LIVE IN A TIME OF SUCH UNPARALLELED ECONOMIC PROSPERITY!

I'LL SAY! MORE HAMBURGER HELPER?

THIS MODERN WORLD

by TOM TOMORROW

OUR TOP STORY TONIGHT: THE GOVERNOR OF *IOWA* LAUNCHES AN AIR STRIKE AGAINST NEW YORK CITY STRONGMAN *RUDY GIULIANI!*

HIS SECURITY FORCES ARE *TERRORIZING* THE REGION'S ETHNIC POOR!

WE *MUST* DEGRADE HIS CAPABILITIES!

CROP DUSTERS RETROFITTED WITH STATE-OF-THE-ART "STEALTH" TECHNOLOGY UNLEASH IOWA'S VAST ARSENAL OF *FARMING BYPRODUCTS* ON THE CITY!

IS THIS WHAT I *THINK* IT IS..?

I'M AFRAID SO, SIR! NOW, PLEASE--WE'VE GOT TO GET YOU TO YOUR *BUNKER!*

DAMN THOSE CORN-EATING IMPERIALISTS!

SPLAT!

SPLAT!

THE ISSUE IS DEBATED ON CABLE ACCESS CHANNELS THROUGHOUT THE STATE!

IF WE IOWANS DON'T SET A MORAL EXAMPLE-- WHO *WILL?*

YES, BUT WHAT'S OUR *END-GAME STRATEGY?* CAN MIDWESTERNERS *REALLY* SOLVE THE PROBLEMS OF A CITY WITH SUCH A LONG HISTORY OF ETHNIC AND RELIGIOUS STRIFE?

GROUND TROOPS MAY EVENTUALLY PROVE NECESSARY-- BUT SO FAR, IOWANS REMAIN ADAMANTLY *OPPOSED* TO THE IDEA...

YOU WOULDN'T GET *ME* NEAR THAT PLACE! NO *WAY!*

IT'S SO DIRTY AND CROWDED! AND PEOPLE DRIVE LIKE *MANIACS!*

MY UNCLE WENT THERE ONCE--AND GOT LOST ON THE SUBWAY FOR *THREE DAYS!*

COMING UP NEXT: WILL HOSTILITIES SPILL OVER INTO NEIGHBORING *NEW JERSEY?* STAY TUNED!

THIS MODERN WORLD
by TOM TOMORROW

 HEY KIDS! IT'S TIME FOR-- **POLITICALLY INCORRECT!**

TONIGHT'S INSIGHTFUL GUESTS INCLUDE--

 --A BLONDE REPUBLICAN PUNDIT--

 --A BURNED-OUT ROCKER--

 --AN EMPTY-HEADED ACTOR-- WINK!

 --AND THE DOG FROM THE TACO BELL ADS! WOOF!

 OUR SUBJECT IS CAMPAIGN FINANCE REFORM: DO WE **NEED** IT? BLONDE REPUBLICAN?

 BILL, THIS IS JUST A **LIBERAL PLOT** TO SHUT THE **RICH** OUT OF **POLITICS!**

SAY, HOW DO YOU LIKE MY **LEGS**? NOT **BAD**, HUH?

 WELL, THEY'RE CERTAINLY BETTER THAN GEORGE WILL'S!

EMPTY-HEADED ACTOR-- WHAT DO **YOU** THINK?

 ABOUT HER LEGS?

DID I SAY SOMETHING **FUNNY**?

HA HA HA HA HA HA

 HEY, BILL-- IF I COULD JUMP IN HERE, MAN-- I REMEMBER WHEN I WAS TOURING BACK IN '70 OR '71-- AND RICHARD NIXON WAS, LIKE--

--PRESIDENT!

IT WAS WEIRD.

 WELL-- OK THEN!

TACO BELL DOG-- DO YOU HAVE ANY DELIGHTFULLY AMUSING QUIPS FOR US?

 BILL, I BELIEVE THAT CAMPAIGN FINANCE REFORM IS **IMPERATIVE** IF WE WANT TO TAKE CONTROL OF OUR DEMOCRACY BACK FROM THE **CORPORATE INTERESTS** WHO—

WHOA! HOLD ON THERE, CHAMP!

 WHAT DO YOU THINK THIS IS-- C-SPAN?

COMING UP NEXT: MORE ABOUT THE BLONDE REPUBLICAN'S **LEGS!**

FIRST, THESE MESSAGES!

THIS MODERN WORLD

by TOM TOMORROW

IT'S ALWAYS NICE TO THINK THERE ARE *EASY* ANSWERS...

I'M GOING TO INVEST ALL MY SAVINGS IN THE VOLATILE *TECH MARKET*-- AND LIVE *HAPPILY EVER AF-TER!*

MY WIFE IS *SURE* TO FORGIVE ME FOR THAT AFFAIR WITH THE BABY-SITTER-- ONCE I GIVE HER THESE LOVELY *ROSES!*

...BUT UNFORTUNATELY, THERE USUALLY *AREN'T*... AND IF YOU GUESSED WE MIGHT BE LEADING UP TO *KOSOVO* HERE, YOU'RE *RIGHT*...

AFTER ALL, THE NATO BOMBINGS-- WHICH WERE SUPPOSED TO QUICK-LY BRING THE SERBS IN LINE-- HAVE INSTEAD MANAGED TO IN-TENSIFY THE ETHNIC CLEANSING, HARDEN MILOSEVIC'S RESERVE, *AND* SET OFF THE WORST REF-UGEE CRISIS EUROPE HAS SEEN SINCE *WORLD WAR II*...

NOW, WE KNOW THAT AT THIS POINT, MANY OF YOU ARE THINKING, "WE HAD TO DO SOME-THING"-- BUT LOOK AT IT THIS WAY--

--IF THE PRESIDENT WERE A *SU-PERHERO*-- JUST GO WITH IT FOR A MOMENT, OKAY?-- AND IN THE COURSE OF HIS NIGHTLY ROUNDS HE HAPPENED ON A *MUGGING*--

GIMME YOUR PURSE, LADY!

OH, DEAR!

--AND HE RESPONDED BY PULLING OUT AN *ASSAULT RIFLE* AND FIRING SEVERAL DOZEN ROUNDS IN THE GENERAL DIRECTION OF THE CRIME-- TAKING OUT THE MUG-GER AND HIS VICTIM *BOTH*--

STOP, FIEND!

RATATATATATAT

URK

AK

--WOULD YOU THEN NOD YOUR HEAD IN APPROVAL AS HE LOOKED DOWN AT THE CARNAGE AND BIT HIS UPPER LIP AND DECLARED IN A HOARSE YET DETERMINED VOICE--

--I HAD TO DO *SOME-THING!*

...WE DIDN'T THINK SO.

TOM TOMORROW©99 • TIP O' THE PEN (GUN) TO NOAM CHOMSKY FOR THE MUGGING ANALOGY...

THIS MODERN WORLD

by TOM TOMORROW

IN RESPONSE TO THE LITTLETON MASSACRE, THE PRESIDENT -- WHO HAS ORDERED THE BOMBING OF FOUR DIFFERENT COUNTRIES SINCE LAST AUGUST -- DECLARED WITH A STRAIGHT FACE THAT--

--WE MUST TEACH OUR CHILDREN TO SETTLE THEIR DIFFERENCES THROUGH *WORDS* AND NOT *WEAPONS!*

...NOW IF YOU'LL EXCUSE ME, I'VE GOT SOME *MISSILES* TO LAUNCH!

CONSERVATIVES, MEANWHILE, THRASHED ABOUT DESPERATELY FOR ANY EXPLANATION OTHER THAN THE *OBVIOUS*...

WE MUST BAN THESE NEW-FANGLED *VIDEOGAMES!* THEY'RE THE *REAL* CULPRIT HERE!

NOT TO MENTION *BLACK TRENCHCOATS!* THIS TRAGEDY *CLEARLY* UNDERSCORES THE NEED FOR *SCHOOL UNIFORMS!**

*ACTUAL CONSERVATIVE RESPONSES.

NOW-- TO ANTICIPATE THE E-MAIL THAT'S ALREADY BEING COMPOSED IN RESPONSE TO THIS CARTOON-- IT'S TRUE THAT WE LIVE IN A SOCIETY SATURATED WITH VIOLENT IMAGES ...AND *IT'S* TRUE THAT THE KILLERS *MIGHT* HAVE INFLICTED SIGNIFICANT DAMAGE WITH THEIR HOMEMADE BOMBS *ALONE*...

...BUT THE KEY TO THESE SHOOTING SPREES IS *STILL* THE READY AVAILABILITY OF THE GODDAMN GUNS *THEMSELVES*...AND UNTIL CONGRESS STOPS KOWTOWING TO THE GUN LOBBY, *THAT'S* JUST NOT GOING TO *CHANGE*...

HOW ABOUT WAITING PERIODS? TRIGGER LOCKS? WARNING LABELS? ANY MEANINGLESS PANACEA *WHATSOEVER?*

NOT IF YOU WANT *OUR* CASH, YOU NAZI.

BONUS *EQUAL TIME* PANEL: CHARLTON HESTON'S REASONS YOU *SHOULD* OWN A GUN (NO. 27 IN A SERIES)!

--BECAUSE YOU NEVER KNOW WHEN YOU'RE GOING TO BE THE LAST HUMAN LIVING ON A PLANET FULL OF *HORRIBLE MUTANTS!*

FORGIVE US, MR. HESTON! WE DID NOT REALIZE YOU POSSESSED SUCH WEAPONRY!

WE WILL NOT BOTHER YOU AGAIN!

TOM TOMORROW © 1999

THIS MODERN WORLD

by TOM TOMORROW

THIS WEEK:

RANDOM SCAPEGOATS for the LITTLETON MASSACRE*

*A PUBLIC SERVICE FOR OUR FRIENDS IN THE N.R.A., WHO HAVE BEEN CASTING ABOUT DESPERATELY FOR ANYTHING TO BLAME OTHER THAN THE READY AVAILABILITY OF HIGH-POWERED WEAPONRY.

1. THE DISAPPOINTING NEW BATCH OF ANIMATED TV SHOWS.

IF THE KILLERS WERE ANTICIPATING A REPRISE OF THE DEFT, INSOUCIANT SATIRE OF THE SIMPSONS--

--THE HEAVY-HANDED SHTICK OF THESE SHOWS MIGHT HAVE DRIVEN THEM OVER THE EDGE!

2. THE PRIVATIZATION OF SOCIAL SECURITY.

HOW CAN POLITICIANS EVEN CONSIDER TYING THE FATE OF OUR NATION'S ELDERLY AND POOR TO THE VAGARIES OF THE STOCK MARKET?

IT'S ENOUGH TO DRIVE ANYONE MAD!

3. TINKY WINKY, THE GAY TELETUBBY.

THE CULTURAL IMPACT OF THIS SEEMINGLY INNOCUOUS CHARACTER SHOULD NOT BE UNDERESTIMATED!

WHO KNOWS WHAT OTHER SUBLIMINAL MESSAGES HE MAY BE DISSEMINATING?

4. THE INCESSANT BLATHER OF THE PUNDITOCRACY.

ALL THEY DO IS TALK AND TALK AND TALK!

COKIE--SAM--THE BELTWAY BOYS-- AND ALL THOSE RIGHT-WING BLONDE CHICKS...I CAN'T GET THEIR VOICES OUT OF MY HEAD!

5. AND OF COURSE, THE OLD FALLBACKS-- BLACK TRENCHCOATS, VIDEOGAMES, AND MARILYN MANSON...

NOT THAT IT MAKES MUCH SENSE TO BLAME THE DEATHS OF 15 PEOPLE ON CLOTHING AND MUSICIANS--

HEY, GUYS-- ANYTHING THAT DRAWS ATTENTION AWAY FROM THE GUNS IS FINE WITH ME!

NRA

54

THIS MODERN WORLD

by TOM TOMORROW

THE LAST JAMES BOND MOVIE FEATURED A RUPERT MURDOCH-LIKE VILLAIN WHO *CREATED* CATASTROPHES FOR HIS MEDIA OUTLETS TO COVER...THE REAL-LIFE CABLE NEWS CHANNELS MAY NOT HAVE GONE *THAT* FAR, BUT THEY *ARE* DISTURBINGLY DEPENDENT ON *TRAGEDIES* AND *DISASTERS*...

"MSNBC *SHATTERED* ITS PREVIOUS QUARTER-HOUR RECORD, SCORING 2,018,000 HOUSEHOLDS DURING JOHN GIBSON'S INTERVIEW WITH A COLUMBINE HIGH SCHOOL STUDENT!"

"*CNN* POSTED TOTAL-DAY INCREASES OF 425 PERCENT IN RATING AND 409 IN DELIVERY, AVERAGING A 2.1 RATING AND DELIVERING *1.6 MILLION HOMES!"*

*EXCERPTS FROM CROWING PRESS RELEASES ISSUED BY CNN AND MSNBC.

GRIEF AND SUFFERING MEAN *BOFFO BOX OFFICE* FOR THESE NETWORKS...AND WHETHER IT'S A SCHOOLYARD SHOOTING OR THE CRASH OF AN AIRLINER, THEY'RE GOING TO SQUEEZE IT FOR *EVERYTHING IT'S WORTH*...

LATER IN THE HALF-HOUR WE'LL TAKE ANOTHER LOOK AT THE SNAZZY LOGO AND THEME MUSIC WE'VE CREATED FOR THE *HIGH SCHOOL HORRORFEST™*!

BUT FIRST--SPECULATION FROM OUR PANEL OF UNQUALIFIED EXPERTS ABOUT THE SEXUAL ORIENTATION AND DIETARY HABITS OF THE *TEENAGE TERRORMONGERS™*!

ABLE NEWS WORK

CABLE McNEWS NETWORK

CAB McNE NETW

OF COURSE, WE'RE *ALL* COMPLICIT IN THIS--FROM THE SURVIVORS WHO STOP TO PROVIDE PITHY, NEWSCAST-READY *SOUND BITES* BEFORE THEY'VE EVEN RECEIVED *PROPER MEDICAL ATTENTION*--

DO YOU HAVE ANYTHING TO SAY TO OUR VIEWERS AT HOME?

YOU BET! I BELIEVE THIS CARNAGE RESULTED FROM A LACK OF *SCHOOL SPIRIT!* ATTENDANCE AT PEP RALLIES SHOULD BE REQUIRED BY *LAW*!

--TO THE VOYEURISTIC NEWS *AUDIENCE*...WHICH BEGINS TO CONFUSE AN ENTIRELY APPROPRIATE RESPONSE OF SYMPATHY AND COMPASSION FOR A SENSE OF *ACTUAL PERSONAL LOSS*...

I'M GOING TO SEND SOME FLOWERS TO--UM --THOSE PEOPLE ON THE TEEVEE!

I AM CERTAIN THE GRIEF AND DEVASTATION I AM EXPERIENCING AS A RESULT OF THE *HIGH SCHOOL HORRORFEST™* WILL REMAIN WITH ME ALWAYS!

OR AT LEAST UNTIL THE *NEXT* EXCITING CABLE NEWS TRAGEDY!

THIS MODERN WORLD

by TOM TOMORROW

TELECOMMUTING IS OFTEN TOUTED AS THE WAVE OF THE FUTURE...IN FACT, TO HEAR THE FUTURISTS TELL IT, THERE'S NO LONGER *ANY* *REASON* TO BE PHYSICALLY PRESENT AT WORK...

OKAY--I WANT TO UNLOAD 3COMM AND IBM--

--AND INVEST *EVERYTHING* IN MR. *BUBBLE!*

WHAT?

OF COURSE, AS ANY FREELANCER CAN ATTEST, WORKING AT HOME IS *WAY* OVERRATED...

--AND SO YOU SEE, I WORK ALONE *ALL DAY LONG!* I *NEVER* LEAVE THE HOUSE! I'M *COMPLETELY STARVED* FOR *BASIC HUMAN INTERACTION!* SAY-- WHAT'S *YOUR* NAME? YOU WANT TO BE FRIENDS? MAYBE WE CAN BE FRIENDS! WHADDYA THINK? HUH? HUH?

UM, WHATEVER. LOOK, YOU WANT FRIES OR NOT?

ALL NEW WACKY BURGER

THINGS GO BETTER WITH Sugar Water

AND ANYWAY-- IF THE TECHNOPHILES IN PLACES LIKE SILICON VALLEY ARE SO CON- VINCED THAT COMPUTERS HAVE LIBERATED US ALL FROM THE CONSTRAINTS OF GEO- GRAPHY--

WHY, YOU COULD WORK IN *CLEVELAND* AND LIVE IN *HAWAII!* YOU COULD WORK IN *NEW HAVEN* AND LIVE IN *BELIZE!* YOU COULD--

OKAY, I GET THE IDEA.

--THEN WHY ARE SO MANY OF *THEM* WILL- ING TO PAY SOME OF THE MOST INFLATED HOUSING PRICES ON THE *PLANET*--IN ORDER TO, WELL, LIVE IN PLACES LIKE *SILICON VALLEY?*

THREE QUARTERS OF A MILLION DOL- LARS FOR A CORRUGATED TIN *TOOL SHED* WITH A *DIRT FLOOR* AND *NO PLUMBING?*

WHAT A BARGAIN! WE'LL *TAKE* IT!

WE'LL BE SO CLOSE TO WORK!

TOM TOMORROW © 99

THIS MODERN WORLD

by TOM TOMORROW

Panel 1: HELLO--I'M *WILLIAM SHATNER!* IN MY BEST-KNOWN ROLE--AS TV POLICEMAN *T.J. HOOKER,* OF COURSE--I OFTEN ARRESTED *CRIMINALS*...BUT TODAY, I'M HERE WITH SOME *ARRESTING* NEWS FOR *YOU* ABOUT *PRICELINE.COM*-- THE WEBSITE THAT TAKES A *BITE* OUT OF AIRLINE PRICES!

Panel 2: YOU SEE, MUCH AS POLICE OFFICERS LIKE *T.J. HOOKER* USE COMPUTER TECHNOLOGY TO APPREHEND LAWBREAKERS, *PRICELINE* USES THE INTER- NET TO APPREHEND THE BEST DEAL FOR *YOU!*

?

Panel 3: AND THIS COMPANY IS HOTTER THAN A STOLEN FERRARI BEING PURSUED BY HEATHER LOCKLEAR AND MYSELF IN ANOTHER EXCITING EPISODE OF *T.J. HOOKER!* WHY, PRICELINE JUST WENT PUBLIC--AND NOW HAS A STREET VALUE OF APPROXIMATELY *TEN BILLION DOLLARS!*

BUT MR. SHATNER--THAT'S MORE THAN SEVERAL MA- JOR AIRLINES *COMBINED!*

Panel 4: HOW CAN AN ELEVEN-MONTH- OLD COMPANY WITH LOSSES OF $114 MILLION--WHICH HAS BEEN SELLING ITS PRODUCT *BELOW COST* TO KEEP CUS- TOMERS HAPPY--*POSSIBLY* BE WORTH SO MUCH? ISN'T THIS JUST FURTHER EVIDENCE OF THE BULL MARKET'S FUN- DAMENTAL *IRRATIONALITY?*

Panel 5: SON--YOU'RE BEING MORE OBTUSE THAN A POLICE COMMISSIONER WITH NOTH- ING BETTER TO DO THAN MAKE LIFE DIFFICULT FOR *T.J. HOOKER!* DIDN'T YOU HEAR THE NAME OF THE COMPANY? IT'S PRICELINE- *DOT-COM!* GET IT? *DOT- COM!* IT'S AN *INTERNET* COMPANY!

Panel 6: OH! WELL THEN IT ALL MAKES *SENSE*...

...I GUESS...

GOOD! NOW AS I MIGHT HAVE SAID AT THE CONCLUSION OF ANOTHER THRILL- PACKED EPISODE OF *T.J. HOOKER,* "BOOK 'EM!"--YOUR *AIRLINE TICK- ETS,* THAT IS! AFTER ALL-- IT WOULD BE A *CRIME* TO MISS OUT ON PRICES LIKE *THESE!*

Panel 7: SO ARE THE SAVINGS *OUT OF THIS WORLD?* IS THIS THE *FINAL FRONTIER* OF AIRLINE TICKET WEB SITES?

KID, I DON'T KNOW WHAT THE HELL YOU'RE TALKING ABOUT.

TOM TOMORROW ©99

THIS MODERN WORLD

by TOM TOMORROW

AS LONGTIME READERS OF THIS CARTOON ARE AWARE, WE OCCASIONALLY END UP WITH SOME LOOSE TIDBITS WE HAVEN'T QUITE MANAGED TO WORK INTO A STRIP... SO THIS WEEK, A LITTLE *HOUSECLEANING*...

SPARKY--ISN'T THIS REALLY JUST AN EXCUSE TO HASTILY SLAP A CARTOON TOGETHER FOR PAPERS TO RUN DURING OUR UPCOMING *VACATION*?

SILLY DOG! IT'S NOT A VACATION--IT'S A TAX-DEDUCTIBLE *FACT-FINDING MISSION!*

NOW, HAVE YOU SEEN THE SUNBLOCK?

FOR INSTANCE... IT SOUNDS LIKE A BAD JOKE, BUT WE SWEAR THIS IS TRUE: WHILE WATCHING DAYTIME T.V. RECENTLY,* WE DISCOVERED THAT *O.J. SIMPSON* IS ONCE AGAIN GAINFULLY EMPLOYED -- AS THE SPOKESMAN FOR SOMETHING CALLED *1-800-LAW-HELP*...

"...BECAUSE THERE'S NOTHING MORE IMPORTANT THAN HAVING THE RIGHT LAWYER ON YOUR SIDE!"

ACTUAL--AND UNDOUBTEDLY HEARTFELT-- QUOTE FROM COMMERCIAL.

*WE WORK HARD, OH YES WE DO.

AND--SPEAKING OF EVIDENCE THAT REALITY IS FREQUENTLY STRANGER THAN SATIRE--YOU MAY HAVE HEARD THAT *PAULA JONES* ALSO HAS A NEW ENDORSEMENT DEAL -- WITH A *PHONE PSYCHIC NETWORK*...

MISS--A POWERFUL & INFLUENTIAL MAN WOULD LIKE TO INVITE YOU UP TO HIS HOTEL ROOM-- TO, UM, DISCUSS YOUR *CAREER PROSPECTS!*

GEE--I DON'T *KNOW*... ...I'D BETTER CALL THE *PAULA JONES PSYCHIC FRIENDS HOTLINE* FOR ADVICE!

FINALLY: IT'S *CONTEST TIME* AGAIN! SEND A POSTCARD (SORRY-- NO EMAIL ENTRIES) WITH YOUR NAME, ADDRESS, AND THE NAME OF THE PAPER WHERE YOU READ THIS CARTOON TO: *TOM TOMORR...*

SORRY-- CONTEST OVER!

...N.Y., N.Y., 10025... ONE LUCKY RECIPIENT-- CHOSEN AT RANDOM--

--WILL RECEIVE THE *ORIGINAL ART* FROM A CLASSIC (I.E., "OLD") TOM TOMORROW CARTOON --SUITABLE FOR DISPLAY IN THE MOST *PROMINENT POSSIBLE SPOT* IN THEIR HOME!*

I LOOK FORWARD TO READING IT OVER AND OVER AGAIN UNTIL I HAVE EVERY SINGLE WORD AND PUNCTUATION MARK *INDELIBLY COMMITTED TO MEMORY!*

HA, HA! BILL CLINTON'S BOXER SHORTS HAVE *HEARTS* ON THEM! AND GET A LOAD OF THIS *CIGAR JOKE!* HOW DOES TOM THINK THIS STUFF *UP?*

HIS CARTOON IS WACKIER THAN A SATURDAY NIGHT LIVE SKETCH!

*3 RUNNERS-UP WILL GET SPARKY *REFRIGERATOR MAGNETS!*

TOM TOMORROW©99• www.thismodernworld.com ... NEW! animated tomorrow online -- www.protocomix.com!

THIS MODERN WORLD

by TOM TOMORROW

WILSON, YOU'VE GOT TO EXPLAIN THIS "GAY REPUBLICAN" THING TO ME.

LOG CABIN CLUB

I MEAN, YOU'VE AFFILIATED YOURSELF WITH A POLITICAL PARTY THAT VIEWS YOUR SEXUAL ORIENTATION AS A DISEASE AT BEST, IF NOT AN OUTRIGHT ABOMINATION AGAINST GOD--

LOG CABIN CLUB

--A PARTY THAT TRIES TO PORTRAY HOMOSEXUALITY AS THE MOST INSIDIOUS THREAT TO AMERICAN SOCIETY SINCE THE COLD WAR!

WHAT COULD YOU POSSIBLY BE THINKING?

LOG CABIN CLUB

UM--I'M IN A HIGH TAX BRACKET.

IMAGINE MY SURPRISE.

I THOUGHT MAYBE YOU'D BEEN WON OVER BY GARY BAUER'S STIRRING RHETORIC...

LOG CABIN CLUB

TOM TOMORROW©99 • www.thismodernworld.com

59

THIS MODERN WORLD

by TOM TOMORROW

HEY, CHUCK! HOW YA DOIN'?

WELL, BIFF--SINCE YOU AND I ARE CASUALLY ACQUAINTED AT BEST, I'LL HAVE TO GLIBLY AND SOMEWHAT INACCURATELY RESPOND WITH A SIMPLE "FINE--AND YOU?"

OH, THE SAME!

BOY, THERE ARE QUITE A LOT OF CONTROVERSIAL POLITICAL EVENTS IN THE NEWS THESE DAYS, AREN'T THERE?

YES, BUT GIVEN THE POTENTIAL FOR CONFLICT AND DISAGREEMENT BETWEEN US, I THINK I'LL QUICKLY STEER THE CONVERSATION TOWARD THE ACCOMPLISHMENTS OF A POPULAR SPORTS TEAM!

THEY CERTAINLY ARE PROFICIENT AT MANIPULATING THE BALL TO THEIR ADVANTAGE, AREN'T THEY?

YES, ALTHOUGH SOME OF THE ATHLETES IN QUESTION HAVE NEGOTIATED A RATE OF COMPENSATION WHICH IS SUBSTANTIALLY DISPROPORTIONATE TO THEIR ABILITIES!

WELL, THERE ARE ANY NUMBER OF THINGS I'D RATHER BE DOING THAN STANDING HERE TALKING TO YOU--SO I GUESS I'LL MUMBLE A FEW MEANINGLESS PLEASANTRIES AND QUICKLY BE ON MY WAY!

YOU GOT THAT RIGHT! BUT HEY-- LET'S DO LUNCH!

THIS MODERN WORLD

by TOM TOMORROW

ACROSS THIS NATION, FROM THE FARMLANDS TO THE SUBURBS, AMERICANS IN SEARCH OF GUIDANCE AND INSIGHT DEPEND ON THE CEASELESS TOIL OF THE EAST COAST MEDIA ELITE!

THE PROBING POLITICAL COMMENTARY OF *HOWARD FINEMAN* IS LIKE A *SHINING BEACON* IN THE FOG OF MY *DREARY EXISTENCE!*

IF NOT FOR THE *CONDÉ NAST* PUBLISHING EMPIRE, *I* WOULDN'T EVEN KNOW WHAT COLOR *NAIL POLISH* TO WEAR!

Newsweak

THROUGHOUT MIDTOWN MANHATTAN, SELFLESS SCRIBES LABOR TIRELESSLY TO KEEP THEIR GEOGRAPHICALLY DISADVANTAGED COUNTRYMEN UP TO DATE ON THE LATEST *NEW YORK CITY STYLE DICTATES...*

HEY, JOE-BOB, I FORGET--ARE SUNGLASSES WITH YELLOW LENSES STILL A DARINGLY OUTRÉ FASHION STATEMENT?

OH FOR HEAVEN'S SAKE, ELMER--DON'T YOU PAY *ANY* ATTENTION TO *DETAILS MAGAZINE?* THOSE GLASSES ARE *SO* 1998!

Details

...WHILE POLITICAL INSIDERS FROM NEW YORK TO WASHINGTON STRIVE TO PUT *CURRENT EVENTS* INTO CONTEXT FOR THEIR *COUNTRY COUSINS...*

HA, HA! LOOK AT THIS! MAUREEN DOWD COMPARES KEN STARR TO *DARTH MAUL!* SHE CALLS HIM-- GET THIS-- *DARTH KEN!*

WITH AN IMAGINATION LIKE THAT, IT IS NO *WONDER* SHE WAS AWARDED A PULITZER PRIZE!

The New York Times

RUSSIANS ENTER KOSOVO EARLY BUT MOSCOW CALLS IT A MISTAKE; BRITISH LEAD

YES, AMERICANS EVERYWHERE CERTAINLY UNDERSTAND THE DEBT OF GRATITUDE THEY OWE THE EASTERN MEDIA ESTABLISHMENT--WITHOUT WHOM, THEY MIGHT NOT *EVER* UNDERSTAND WHAT'S *TRULY IMPORTANT...*

I JUST COULDN'T GET TO *SLEEP* LAST NIGHT AFTER READING HOW HARD IT IS TO FIND PARKING IN MANHATTAN!

IT IS AN OUTRAGE! IF WE CAN PUT A MAN ON THE *MOON,* THEN *WHY* CAN'T WE FIND A WAY TO MAKE LIFE EASIER FOR UPPER MIDDLE CLASS PROFESSIONALS IN *NEW YORK CITY?*

THIS MODERN WORLD

by TOM TOMORROW

Panel 1: LIKE MANY MODERN COUPLES, THEY RELIED HEAVILY ON *SARCASM* AND *IRONIC DETACHMENT*.

ALLY M^CBEAL IS CERTAINLY AN *INSIGHTFUL* AND *ENTERTAINING* TELEVISION PROGRAM.

OH YES--AND VONDA SHEPHERD IS THE MOST *SOULFUL* SINGER I HAVE *EVER HEARD*.

Panel 2: GRADUALLY, THEIR ABILITY TO EXPRESS GENUINE ENTHUSIASM BEGAN TO *ATROPHY* FROM DISUSE.

WHY DON'T WE GO TO BED EARLY AND HAVE *WILD SEX*?

I CAN'T THINK OF ANYTHING I'D *RATHER DO*.

WELL, IF YOU DON'T *WANT* TO--

NO--WAIT--I--SPUTTER--

Panel 3: ONE DAY THEY REALIZED THEY WERE NO LONGER CAPABLE OF COMMUNICATING WITH EACH OTHER.

YOU'RE THE MOST *WONDERFUL PERSON* I KNOW. I *REALLY* MEAN IT.

YOU'RE *SO SWEET*. I JUST *COULDN'T* IMAGINE LIFE *WITHOUT* YOU.

UH OH...

Panel 4: IT WAS ANOTHER MARRIAGE DESTROYED--BY *COMPULSIVE SARCASTIC DISORDER*.

I'M *CERTAINLY* GOING TO MISS YOU.

OH YES--AND I'LL MISS *YOU* AS WELL.

I MEAN--I *REALLY WILL*--

OH, NEVER MIND.

TOM TOMORROW ©99

THIS MODERN WORLD

by TOM TOMORROW

SINCE THE SHOOTING OF AMADOU DIALLO, POLICE-COMMUNITY RELATIONS HAVE BEEN FRAYED IN NEW YORK CITY... CIVILIANS HAVE PROTESTED THE SHOOTING--WHILE *POLICE* HAVE DEMONSTRATED AGAINST THE *PROTESTS*...

I DON'T SEE WHY THEY HAVE TO MAKE SUCH A BIG *DEAL* ABOUT FIRING 41 BULLETS AT AN UNARMED GUY STANDING IN HIS DOORWAY!

IT REALLY HURTS *MY FEELINGS!*

BENEATH OUR HARDENED EXTERIORS WE ARE ACTUALLY QUITE *SENSITIVE*, YOU KNOW!

FORTUNATELY, MAYOR GIULIANI HAS TAKEN *BOLD, DECISIVE ACTION* IN THE MATTER-- BY ORDERING POLICE OFFICERS TO *BE MORE COURTEOUS* TO THE PUBLIC!

IT'S LIKE MISS MANNERS ALWAYS SAYS--

--JUST BECAUSE YOU HAVE SOMEONE IN A CHOKE HOLD, THERE'S NO REASON TO BE *IMPOLITE!*

AS IF THAT WEREN'T *ENOUGH*, N.Y.C. POLICE HAVE ALSO BEEN ISSUED WALLET-SIZED *COURTESY CARDS*--INSTRUCTING THEM TO ADDRESS CITIZENS WITH WHOM THEY INTERACT IN AN *APPROPRIATELY POLITE MANNER!*

UP AGAINST THE FREAKING WALL OR I'LL BLOW YOUR FREAKING HEAD OFF, MY GOOD FELLOW!

AND IF IT'S NOT TOO MUCH BOTHER, WOULD YOU BE SO KIND AS TO KEEP YOUR FREAKING HANDS WHERE WE CAN SEE THEM?

THE CARDS *ALSO* INSTRUCT OFFICERS TO "EXPLAIN TO THE PUBLIC IN A COURTEOUS, PROFESSIONAL DEMEANOR THE REASON FOR YOUR INTERACTION WITH THEM"--*AND* TO "APOLOGIZE FOR ANY INCONVENIENCE"!

...YOU SEE, AS A YOUNG AFRICAN-AMERICAN IN AN IMPOVERISHED NEIGHBORHOOD, YOU'RE SIMPLY SUBJECT TO RANDOM SEARCHES AND HARASSMENT FOR NO APPARENT REASON!

NO PROBLEM, OFFICERS! YOUR COURTEOUS PROFESSIONALISM HAS ALLAYED *ANY* LINGERING RESENTMENT I MIGHT HAVE EXPERIENCED AS A RESULT OF YOUR *THUGGISH BEHAVIOR!*

IT JUST GOES TO SHOW YOU--*POLITENESS COUNTS!*

THIS MODERN WORLD

by TOM TOMORROW

ACCORDING TO TOM DeLAY, SCHOOLYARD MASSACRES HAVE LESS TO DO WITH THE PRESENCE OF *GUNS* IN SCHOOLS THAN THE ABSENCE OF THE *TEN COMMANDMENTS*.

YO, CHECK THIS OUT! GOD SAYS KILLING IS A *SIN*!

WELL, I GUESS THAT RULES OUT OUR *SHOOTING SPREE*! YOU WANNA GO DO SOME VOLUNTEER WORK AT THE OLD FOLK'S HOME INSTEAD?

The Ten Commandments

BUT IF WE LIVE IN SUCH A GODLESS, SECULAR SOCIETY, WHY IS IT THAT MOST POLITICIANS CAN'T OPEN THEIR *MOUTHS* WITHOUT INVOKING THEIR *RELIGIOUS BELIEFS*?

--AND MY FAITH IN JESUS CHRIST *COMPELS* ME TO VOTE FOR A CAPITAL GAINS TAX CUT!

JESUS WOULD BE PROUD OF YOU, SENATOR!

AND WHY ARE DECLARATIONS OF DEEP AND ABIDING FAITH AS MUCH OF A REQUIREMENT FOR PRESIDENTIAL CANDIDATES AS *U.S. CITIZENSHIP*?

--AND DID I MENTION MY COMMITMENT TO CHRISTIAN VALUES SUCH AS *MONOGAMY*--AND, UM, *NOT CHEATING ON MY WIFE*?

NOW THAT I'M OVER 40, I AM A *GOOD CHURCH-GOING CITIZEN*! EVEN IF THOSE RUMORS ABOUT MY PAST ARE TRUE, THEY *NO LONGER MATTER*! NOT THAT I'M ADMITTING ANYTHING!

AL "NOT BILL CLINTON" GORE

Holy Bible

GEORGE W. "NOT A PARTY BOY" BUSH

Holy Bible

AFTER ALL, IF THIS WERE *TRULY* A GODLESS, SECULAR SOCIETY, WOULDN'T OUR POLITICIANS --WELL-- *BEHAVE ACCORDINGLY*?

I THINK PEOPLE WHO INTERPRET THE BIBLE *LITERALLY* ARE *SUPERSTITIOUS MORONS*!

I AM A FOLLOWER OF THE ARCHANGEL URIEL, SENT TO PREPARE HUMANITY FOR THE ARRIVAL OF THE UNARIAN *SPACE BROTHERS*!

SO! WHO WANTS TO TALK ABOUT *FISCAL POLICY*?

BRADLEY 2000

LIDDY

THIS MODERN WORLD

by TOM TOMORROW

THIS MODERN WORLD

by TOM TOMORROW

THIS WEEK: A PEEK INTO THE CRYSTAL BALL AT...

THE PRIMARY SEASON

FEBRUARY, 2000.

TONIGHT IN NEW HAMPSHIRE, THE ANOINTED FRONT RUNNER OF THE PARTY IN QUESTION SUFFERED AN UN-EXPECTED DEFEAT AT THE HANDS OF A DARK HORSE CANDIDATE!

IS HE FINISHED? WILL THE DARK HORSE CANDIDATE BE OUR NEXT PRESIDENT? THIS RACE IS SURE TURN-ING INTO A KNUCK-LE-BITER, EH, WANDA?

APRIL.

WELL, THE FRONT RUNNER SEEMS TO HAVE THE NOMINA-TION LOCKED UP AF-TER ALL, BIFF! THE VOTERS REALLY SEEM TO RESPECT HIS FUND-RAISING PROWESS!

YES--BUT WE STILL HAVE TO ANALYZE HIS CHANCES AGAINST THE OTHER PAR-TY'S ANOINTED FRONT RUNNER! IF YOU ASK ME, IT DOESN'T GET MORE EXCITING THAN THIS!

JUNE.

THE FRONT RUNNER SURE MADE A GAFFE ON THE LARRY KING SHOW TONIGHT, BIFF! THERE'S SIMPLY NO TELLING WHAT WILL HAPPEN NOW!

YES--CONFUSING TAJIKI-STAN WITH TURKMENISTAN COULD COST HIM THE NOM-INATION! I DON'T KNOW ABOUT YOU, BUT THE SUS-PENSE IS JUST KILLING ME!

AUGUST.

--AND SO THE ANOINTED FRONT RUNNER WAS NOMINATED TONIGHT AS HIS PARTY'S CANDIDATE FOR PRESIDENT.

I DON'T THINK ANY-ONE COULD HAVE FORE-SEEN THAT OUTCOME, WANDA--NOT WITH A POLITICAL PROCESS AS FUNDAMENTALLY UN-PREDICTABLE AS OURS!

THIS MODERN WORLD

by TOM TOMORROW

Panel 1:

YOU'VE PROBABLY HEARD THAT THE KANSAS BOARD OF EDUCATION HAS VOTED TO "DISCOURAGE" THE TEACHING OF EVOLUTION TO THAT STATE'S *SCHOOLCHILDREN*...

THAT'S RIGHT! WE DON'T WANT TO *CONFUSE* THEM WITH *CRAZY THEORIES*!

THE FOSSIL RECORD WAS PLANTED BY *SATAN* TO *DECEIVE* US, YOU KNOW!*

*ACTUAL CREATIONIST ARGUMENT.

Panel 2:

...BUT HAVE THEY GONE *FAR ENOUGH*? AFTER ALL, THE INSIDIOUS MENACE OF SECULAR HUMANISM HAS UNDOUBTEDLY SPREAD *THROUGHOUT* THE KANSAS SCHOOL SYSTEM -- LIKE SOME TERRIBLE *LIBERAL CANCER*!

Panel 3:

FOR INSTANCE, STATE EDUCATORS *OBVIOUSLY* NEED TO REVAMP SUBJECTS SUCH AS *ASTRONOMY* AND *GEOLOGY* AS SOON AS *POSSIBLE*...

GOD LIVES UP HERE -- AND THE DEVIL LIVES DOWN *HERE*.

AND THAT'S ALL YOU NEED TO KNOW.

HEAVEN

EARTH

HELL

Panel 4:

AND CLEARLY THE *SOCIAL STUDIES* CURRICULUM NEEDS TO BE PURGED OF ANY EXTRANEOUS *FOOLISHNESS* -- SO TEACHERS CAN FOCUS ON WHAT'S *REALLY* IMPORTANT...

SO YOU SEE, CHILDREN, THE JEWS AND HEATHENS IN ALL THOSE STRANGE, FOREIGN LANDS FAR, FAR AWAY FROM KANSAS --

-- ARE ALL GOING STRAIGHT TO *HELL*! AND THERE'S NOTHING ANYBODY CAN DO ABOUT IT!

ANY QUESTIONS?

Panel 5:

AND THEN THERE'S *GYM CLASS*...WHY RISK EXPOSING YOUNG KANSANS TO SUCH SECULAR DIVERSIONS AS *BASEBALL* AND *FOOTBALL* -- WHEN A WHOLESOME AND EDUCATIONAL *PASSION PLAY RE-ENACTMENT* WILL PROVIDE *ALL* THE EXERCISE THEY *NEED*...

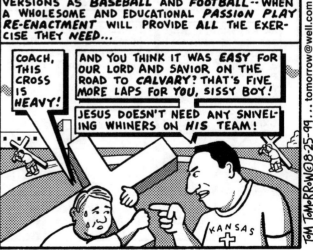

COACH, THIS CROSS IS *HEAVY*!

AND YOU THINK IT WAS *EASY* FOR OUR LORD AND SAVIOR ON THE ROAD TO *CALVARY*? THAT'S FIVE MORE LAPS FOR *YOU*, SISSY BOY!

JESUS DOESN'T NEED ANY SNIVELING WHINERS ON *HIS* TEAM!

KANSAS

THIS MODERN WORLD

by TOM TOMORROW

BACK IN THE OLD DAYS, IF YOU WANTED TO STRIKE IT RICH IN YOUR TWENTIES, YOU HAD TO START A *ROCK BAND* OR SOMETHING.

AND IT WASN'T *EASY,* EITHER! WE HAD TO TAKE LOTS OF DRUGS AND SLEEP WITH STRANGE GIRLS ALMOST *EVERY NIGHT!*

THESE KIDS TODAY DON'T KNOW THE *MEANING* OF HARD WORK!

TIMES HAVE CHANGED...THESE DAYS--IF YOU BELIEVE WHAT YOU READ--ANYONE WHO CAN TURN ON A *COMPUTER* IS PRETTY MUCH *GUARANTEED* TO HIT THE JACKPOT.

I WORKED FOR MICROSOFT FOR *TWO WEEKS*--AND THEN RETIRED TO LIVE OFF MY *STOCK OPTIONS!*

I JUST SOLD MY PAMELA ANDERSON WEBSITE TO AN INVESTMENT CONSORTIUM FOR *THIRTY FIVE MILLION DOLLARS!*

AND OF COURSE, THERE'S ALWAYS *DAY TRADING*-- WHICH, TO JUDGE FROM THE COMMERCIALS, IS LIKE HAVING A LICENSE TO *PRINT MONEY*...

HA, HA, SNOOTY MIDDLE CLASS PERSON! I MAY LOOK LIKE A SCRUFFY SKATE PUNK--BUT THANKS TO *E*TRADE,* I AM ACTUALLY RICH BEYOND YOUR WILDEST DREAMS OF AVARICE!

WELL THEN--I GUESS THE JOKE'S ON *ME!* IF ONLY I HAD KNOWN ABOUT THIS ONLINE GATE TO SUREFIRE WEALTH *SOONER!*

IN FACT, IF YOU'RE UNDER THIRTY AND *HAVEN'T* MADE YOUR FIRST MILLION YET--WELL, WHAT ARE YOU, SOME KIND OF PATHETIC UNDERACHIEVING *LOSER?*

YOU REALIZE THAT THIS ENTIRE ECONOMY IS A CASTLE MADE OF SAND WHICH WILL COME CRASHING DOWN AT THE FIRST HINT OF STORMY WEATHER.

WHAT AN EVOCATIVE METAPHOR! THAT ENGLISH DEGREE MUST *REALLY* COME IN HANDY!

WELL, I'M OFF TO *BARBADOS!*

THIS MODERN WORLD

by TOM TOMORROW

BIFF, I CAN'T BELIEVE YOU'VE **NEVER VOTED**!

WELL, SPARKY, I BELIEVE MY **UTTER APATHY** ACTUALLY HELPS TO MAKE THINGS **BETTER**!

SAY WHAT?

YOU HEARD ME! BY PAYING **NO ATTENTION WHATSOEVER** TO THE PROBLEMS OF THE WORLD, I AM HELPING TO **SOLVE** THEM!

I'M NOT SURE I FOLLOW YOUR **LOGIC** HERE...

YOU KNOW-- IT'S LIKE THEY USED TO SAY IN THE **SIXTIES**--

--IF YOU'RE NOT PART OF THE **PROBLEM**, YOU'RE PART OF THE **SOLUTION**!

UM, THAT'S NOT EXACTLY--

OF COURSE, I WOULDN'T EXPECT A CONFORMIST LIKE **YOU** TO UNDERSTAND MY **RADICAL WORLDVIEW**!

NOW IF YOU'LL EXCUSE ME, I'M GOING TO GO WATCH **JERRY SPRINGER**!

ACTION NEWS: 2099

BROUGHT TO YOU BY THE MS-ABCNNBCBS-FOX NEWS NETWORK

OUR TOP STORY TONIGHT: THE WORLD'S TWO REMAINING CORPORATE CONGLOMERATES HAVE *MERGED*, CREATING A SINGLE MEGALITHIC GLOBAL ENTITY THAT WILL CONTROL *EVERY ASPECT* OF HUMAN COMMERCE! PRETTY EXCITING, EH, WANDA?

IT SURE IS, BIFF! AND, FORTUNATELY, FED CHAIRMAN AND ABSOLUTE RULER *ALAN GREENSPAN* REACTED *FAVORABLY* TO THE MERGER, ACCORDING TO HIGH PRIESTS AT THE *FEDERAL RESERVE TEMPLE!*

CONSOLIDATION EQUALS *EFFICIENCY!* RESISTANCE IS *FUTILE!*

IN OTHER NEWS, SEVERAL HERETICS WERE BURNED AT THE STAKE IN THE INDEPENDENT THEOCRACY OF *KANSAS* TODAY! APPARENTLY THE HERETICS BELIEVED--GET THIS--THAT *PEOPLE* DESCENDED FROM *MONKEYS*!

SHEESH! WELL, SPEAKING OF *BURNING UP*, LET'S CHECK IN WITH METEOROLOGIST *SUNNY DAZE*!

TEMPERATURES ARE *COOL* FOR FEBRUARY, WANDA, HOLDING STEADY IN THE 120-DEGREE RANGE! IT WOULD BE A GREAT DAY FOR A *PICNIC*--EXCEPT, OF COURSE, THAT THE *RADIATION* UP THERE WOULD MELT YOUR BRAIN WITHIN *MINUTES*!

AND, ANYWAY, IF YOU WENT ABOVE GROUND *NOW*, YOU'D MISS BIFF'S DAILY *GUN-MASSACRE UPDATE*! HA, HA!

HA, HA! THANKS, SUNNY! FOLKS, WE'VE GOT REPORTS OF RAMPAGES THROUGHOUT THE NORTHEAST-CORRIDOR SHELTER NETWORK, WITH A FLURRY OF DISGRUNTLED *E-MAIL WORKERS* IN OLD NEW YORK, AS WELL AS SCATTERED *SCHOOL-YARD SLAUGHTERS* IN NEW OLD NEW ENGLAND! IF YOU'RE LEAVING YOUR BUNKER TODAY, WEAR THAT FLAK JACKET AND *KEEP LOW*!

ALL RIGHT, THEN! WE'LL BE BACK AFTER THESE INFORMATIVE PUBLIC-SERVICE MESSAGES EXTOLLING THE VIRTUES OF CONSUMER PRODUCTS *YOU* CAN PURCHASE!

REMEMBER, OUR THRIVING ECONOMY IS *EVERYONE'S* RESPONSIBILITY! MANDATORY CONSUMPTION ISN'T JUST A GOOD IDEA--IT'S THE *LAW*!

TOM TOMORROW ©'99

(ORIGINALLY APPEARED IN *THE NEW YORKER*.)

THIS MODERN WORLD

by TOM TOMORROW

I'M JUST SO BROKEN UP WITH GRIEF OVER THE DEATHS OF JFK, JR. AND THE OTHERS, SPARKY-- I HAVEN'T FELT THIS DISCONSOLATE SINCE--

LET ME GUESS-- THE DEATH OF PRINCESS DI?

UH, YEAH-- THAT'S RIGHT...

LOOK, IT'S CERTAINLY SAD WHEN SOMEONE IS CUT DOWN IN THEIR PRIME-- BUT YOU DIDN'T KNOW THESE PEOPLE! YOU PROBABLY WOULDN'T HAVE RECOGNIZED THEM IF YOU'D SEEN THEM WALKING DOWN THE STREET!

I SUPPOSE YOU FIND THIS TRAGEDY AMUSING IN SOME CYNICAL WAY.

NO, OF COURSE NOT! BUT I DO THINK THIS VICARIOUS GRIEF OF YOURS ONLY CHEAPENS THE REAL GRIEF OF THEIR FAMILY AND FRIENDS! ANYONE WHO'S EVER ACTUALLY LOST SOMEONE SHOULD UNDERSTAND THAT!

AND DID WE REALLY NEED 24-HOUR CABLE NEWS COVERAGE TO INFORM US AS EACH PIECE OF DEBRIS WASHED ASHORE? TELEPHOTO SPY SHOTS OF THE HYANNISPORT COMPOUND? MY GOD, CNN HAD UNDERWATER CAMERAS AT THE SITE! DID THEY HOPE TO CAPTURE FOOTAGE OF THE BODIES BEING RECOVERED? THIS ISN'T GRIEF-- IT'S NECROPHILIA!

BUT SPARKY--DON'T YOU UNDERSTAND? JFK, JR. WAS A CELEBRITY! I FREQUENTLY SAW HIS PHOTOGRAPH IN MAGAZINES!

I'M SORRY. I DON'T KNOW HOW I COULD HAVE BEEN SO INSENSITIVE TO YOUR SUFFERING. SHALL WE TURN ON CNN AND SEE IF THEY'VE GOT ANY UNDERWATER FOOTAGE OF THE WRECKAGE YET?

NOW YOU'RE MAKING SENSE!

THIS MODERN WORLD

by TOM TOMORROW

Panel 1:

THESE DAYS, IT SEEMS LIKE A LOT OF PEOPLE ARE TRYING TO TALK ABOUT RACE WITHOUT MENTIONING *RACE*...

THIS CITY IS A MESS--AND IT'S ALL THE FAULT OF THOSE--UM-- YOU KNOW!

BUT AREN'T THEY JUST VICTIMS OF ECONOMIC CIRCUMSTANCE--I MEAN-- THE, UM, PEOPLE TO WHOM YOU REFER?

Panel 2:

...WHICH HAS LED TO AN UPSWING IN THE USE OF CERTAIN *EUPHEMISMS*, SUCH AS *"INNER CITY"* --OR THE EVER-POPULAR *"AT RISK YOUTH."*

OH MY GOD! THAT YOUTH IS REALLY AT RISK!

WHAT ARE YOU TALKING ABOUT? ALL I SEE IS THAT LITTLE WHITE KID IN FRONT OF THE *SPEEDING CAR*--

--OH.

SCREECH!

71872

Panel 3:

...NOT TO MENTION *"URBAN"*... FOR INSTANCE, WHEN A STARBUCKS RECENTLY OPENED IN *HARLEM*, THE COMPANY PROUDLY ANNOUNCED THAT IT WAS THEIR FIRST "URBAN" STORE...

--AND SO ALL THOSE OTHER STARBUCKS IN MAJOR CITIES ACROSS THE COUNTRY--?

WELL, THEY'RE IN CITIES-- BUT THEY ARE NOT "URBAN"-- IF YOU KNOW WHAT I MEAN! THEY'RE "MIDDLE CLASS"-- IF YOU GET MY DRIFT! THEIR CUSTOMERS ARE NOT "AT RISK"-- IF YOU SEE WHAT I --

STOP IT. YOU'RE MAKING MY HEAD HURT.

Panel 4:

AND THEN THERE'S THE MATTER OF *POLICE PROFILING*...WHICH, THE COPS INSIST, HAS *NOTHING* TO DO WITH *RACE*...

WE'RE JUST LOOKING FOR *AT RISK, INNER CITY, URBAN YOUTH!*

IT'S NOT *OUR* FAULT IF THEY HAPPEN TO BE *BLACK!*

73

THIS MODERN WORLD

by TOM TOMORROW

IT'S TIME FOR YET ANOTHER CABLE TV *CELEBRITY BIOGRAPHY!* FIRST, WE GLIMPSE THE DIFFICULT EARLY YEARS...

SPARKY NEVER DID REALLY FIT IN AROUND HERE.

HE WAS AN ODD ONE, THAT PENGUIN. ALWAYS COMPLAINING.

AND WHAT WAS THE DEAL WITH THOSE *SHADES,* ANYWAY?

...THEN, THE METEORIC RISE TO STARDOM...

--AND WHEN *THE WRATH OF SPARKY* WAS PUBLISHED, WE MUST HAVE BEEN SELLING TWO OR THREE COPIES A *WEEK!* I'D NEVER SEEN ANYTHING *LIKE* IT!

AT LEAST, UM, IN TERMS OF OBSCURE ALTERNATIVE WEEKLY CARTOON COMPILATIONS.

SO AM I GONNA BE ON TV?

STAR WARS DIET PLAN

STAR WARS GUIDE TO BETTER SEX

STAR WARS EXERCISE PLAN

$00.00

Welcome to Your Friendly Neighborhood **CORPORATE BOOKSTORE**™ SERVING YOUR NEEDS WITH CENTRALIZED EFFICIENCY SINCE 1997

HELLO MAY I HELP YOU?

...FOLLOWED, OF COURSE, BY THE INEVITABLE *DOWNWARD SPIRAL.*

HEY! ONE OF YOU HO'S GET ME SOME MORE FRESH HERRING--AND I MEAN *NOW!*

I'M SPARKY THE *WONDER PENGUIN,* DAMMIT!

(A RE-ENACTMENT)

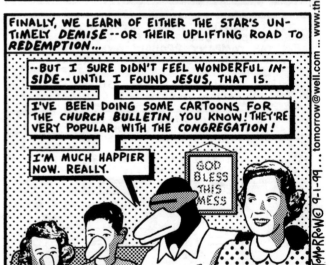

FINALLY, WE LEARN OF EITHER THE STAR'S UNTIMELY *DEMISE*--OR THEIR UPLIFTING ROAD TO *REDEMPTION...*

--BUT I SURE DIDN'T FEEL WONDERFUL *INSIDE*--UNTIL I FOUND *JESUS,* THAT IS.

I'VE BEEN DOING SOME CARTOONS FOR THE *CHURCH BULLETIN,* YOU KNOW! THEY'RE VERY POPULAR WITH THE *CONGREGATION!*

I'M MUCH HAPPIER NOW. REALLY.

GOD BLESS THIS MESS

TOM TOMORROW© 9-1-99...tomorrow@well.com...www.thismodernworld.com

THIS MODERN WORLD

by TOM TOMORROW

Panel 1:

GOVERNOR BUSH, HAVE YOU EVER HAD SEX WITH UNDERAGE MALE PROSTITUTES WHILE DRESSED IN YOUR MOTHER'S *UNDERGARMENTS*?

ABSOLUTELY NOT! I DON'T KNOW HOW THESE RUMORS GET *STARTED*!

Panel 2:

GOVERNOR, IS IT TRUE YOU ONCE SHOT A MAN IN RENO JUST TO WATCH HIM *DIE*?

OF *COURSE* NOT! YOU SHOULD BE ASHAMED OF YOURSELF FOR EVEN *REPEATING* SUCH SCURRILOUS GOSSIP!

Panel 3:

GOVERNOR, HAVE YOU REJECTED YOUR CHRISTIAN FAITH IN FAVOR OF DARK SATANIC RITUALS INVOLVING ANIMAL SACRIFICE AND OTHER *UNSPEAKABLE* ACTS?

GOOD HEAVENS, NO! THIS OUTRAGEOUS SLANDER IS *CLEARLY* THE WORK OF MY POLITICAL ADVERSARIES!

Panel 4:

GOVERNOR, ONE MORE QUESTION-- HAVE YOU EVER USED *COCAINE*?

Panel 5:

Panel 6:

LOOK, HOW MANY TIMES DO I HAVE TO *TELL* YOU PEOPLE? I'M *NOT* GOING TO ANSWER ANY QUESTIONS ABOUT WHAT I MAY OR MAY NOT HAVE DONE TWENTY YEARS AGO!

AT LEAST, NOT ON THAT SPECIFIC SUBJECT!

AND I CATEGORICALLY MAY OR MAY NOT HAVE DANCED NAKED ON ANY *TABLETOPS*!

I HAVE TO GO NOW.

THIS MODERN WORLD

by TOM TOMORROW

THE ECONOMY IS SUPPOSEDLY SKYROCKETING -- YET MORE THAN TWO-THIRDS OF AMERICANS SAY THEY FEEL COMPLETELY LEFT BEHIND.

WHAT IS THE POINT OF LIVING IF YOU DO NOT HAVE STOCK OPTIONS?

IT IS A HOLLOW EXISTENCE INDEED.

SO MAYBE YOU'RE FEELING A LITTLE *DISEN-FRANCHISED*...AND MAYBE YOU'RE LOOKING FOR SOMEONE TO *BLAME*...

IT'S THE LIBERALS IN WASHINGTON -- SPENDING ALL OUR MONEY ON FREE *PARTIAL BIRTH ABORTIONS* FOR *SECULAR HUMANISTS!*

NO, DON'T YOU SEE? IT'S THE BABY BOOMER CABAL, CONSPIRING AGAINST GEN X-- LIKE THEY ALWAYS DO!

THERE'S CERTAINLY NO SHORTAGE OF SCAPEGOATS OUT THERE...IN FACT YOU'RE REALLY ONLY LIMITED BY YOUR OWN *IMAGINATION*...

IT'S OBVIOUS THAT THE *CANADIANS* ARE SECRETLY MANIPULATING OUR ECONOMY FOR THEIR OWN NEFARIOUS PURPOSES! ANY *MORON* CAN SEE THAT!

NO--IT'S THOSE DAMNED MEDDLESOME *SPACE ALIENS* BOMBARDING WALL STREET WITH THEIR INVISIBLE *MIND CONTROL* RAYS! WHY CAN'T THEY JUST LEAVE US *ALONE*?

MEANWHILE, THERE'S A ROOMFUL OF CEO'S SOMEWHERE LAUGHING THEIR ASSES OFF AT YOU.

ONE PERCENT OF THE POPULATION CONTROLS FORTY PERCENT OF THE WEALTH -- AND THESE MORONS CAN'T FIGURE IT OUT!

I'LL HAVE MY MEDIA OUTLETS RUN SOME MORE STORIES ABOUT HOW EASY IT IS TO GET RICH THESE DAYS! THAT'LL *REALLY* MESS WITH THEIR HEADS!

IS THIS A GREAT COUNTRY OR WHAT?

TOM TOMORROW © 9-15-99 ... tomorrow@well.com ... www.thismodernworld.com

THIS MODERN WORLD

by TOM TOMORROW

FEW PEOPLE ARE AWARE THAT AN *EVIL GEORGE W. BUSH* SOMEHOW CROSSED OVER FROM A *MIRROR UNIVERSE* SEVERAL YEARS BACK...

HEH, HEH! IF I SHAVE OFF *MY BEARD*, EVERYONE WILL THINK I AM *HIM*!

...AND HE'S BEEN KEEPING HIMSELF BUSY EVER *SINCE*, ENGAGING IN A *VARIETY* OF *UNSEEMLY ACTIVITIES*...

WOO HOO! IT'S ME, GEORGE W. BUSH--BREAKING THE SPEED LIMIT! I'M OFF TO MAKE MORE QUESTIONABLE BUSINESS DEALS ON THE STRENGTH OF MY FATHER'S *CONNECTIONS*!

THAT DOES NOT SOUND LIKE THE GEORGE W. BUSH I HAVE READ ABOUT!

BUT WHO ELSE COULD IT HAVE BEEN-- SOME *EVIL IMPOSTER*?

...LEAVING A TRAIL OF *RUMORS* AND *INNUENDO* TO BESMIRCH HIS COUNTERPART'S *GOOD NAME*.

HOO BOY! THERE'S NOTHING I LOVE AS MUCH AS DANCING *NAKED* ON A *TABLETOP*! SWING *FREE*, LITTLE GEORGE W!

SIR, THIS ISN'T A GOOD IDEA.

AW, LOOSEN UP! SAY, DIDJA HEAR THE ONE ABOUT THE DEATH ROW *INMATE* PLEADING FOR HER *LIFE*?

MEANWHILE--SINCE NO ONE WOULD EVER BELIEVE THE TRUTH--THE *REAL* GEORGE W. BUSH HAS BEEN FORCED TO TAKE *DRASTIC MEASURES*.

RAISING THIS MUCH MONEY WILL MAKE ME LOOK LIKE I'M BEHOLDEN TO CORPORATE INTERESTS --BUT WITH *HIM* OUT THERE, I HAVE NO *CHOICE*!

DON'T WORRY, SIR-- I DON'T EXPECT ANYTHING IN RETURN! I JUST WANT THE AMERICAN PEOPLE TO SEE YOU FOR THE GOOD AND DECENT MAN YOU *ARE*!

WILL DUBYA DEFEAT HIS *EVIL TWIN*? STAY TUNED!

TOM TOMORROW© 9-8-99 ... tomorrow@well.com ... www.thismodernworld.com

77

THIS MODERN WORLD

by TOM TOMORROW

Panel 1:
SO WHY DO YOU LIBERAL ELIT-ISTS SPEND SO MUCH TIME WORRY-ING ABOUT GUNS, ANYWAY? CARS KILL PLENTY OF PEOPLE, YOU KNOW! I DON'T HEAR YOU BLATHERING ON ABOUT THE NEED FOR *CAR CONTROL!*

Panel 2:
UM, YES, GOOD POINT, BIFF. EXCEPT THAT YOU'RE COMPARING A DEVICE WHICH IS *DESIGNED* TO KILL-- AND INDEED, HAS NO OTHER REAL FUNCTION-- TO A MODE OF TRANS-PORTATION WHICH ONLY RESULTS IN FATALITIES WHEN AN *ACCIDENT* OCCURS.

Panel 3:
AND YOU DO UNDERSTAND THAT, UNLIKE GUNS, CARS *ARE* HEAV-ILY REGULATED--THROUGH VE-HICLE REGISTRATION, DRIVER'S LICENSING, AND THE ENFORCEMENT OF TRAFFIC AND SPEEDING LAWS? IF GUNS HAD *HALF* AS MUCH OVERSIGHT, WE WOULDN'T BE *HAVING* THIS CONVERSATION!

Panel 4:
BUT LET ME GUESS--IT MADE SENSE WHEN RUSH SAID IT.

Panel 5:

Panel 6:
WELL, WHAT ABOUT LARGE *ROCKS*, MR. SMARTY PANTS? THE COLUM-BINE KILLERS COULD HAVE JUST AS EASILY KILLED ALL THOSE PEOPLE WITH *ROCKS!* NEXT, I SUPPOSE YOU'LL WANT *ROCK CONTROL!*

BIFF, I JUST CAN'T AR-GUE WITH LOGIC LIKE THAT...

TOM TOMORROW@9-22-99... tomorrow@well.com ... www.thismodernworld.com

THIS MODERN WORLD

by TOM TOMORROW

THIS MODERN WORLD

by TOM TOMORROW

AT THE MOMENT HE IS POISED TO BECOME A POWER-FUL POLITICAL SPOILER, PAT BUCHANAN REITERATES HIS OFT-STATED BELIEF THAT ADOLF HITLER'S IN-TENTIONS WERE *MISUNDERSTOOD.*

THIS IS *CERTAIN* TO BROADEN MY BASE OF SUP-PORT!

NOTHING RESONATES WITH AMERICAN VOTERS LIKE AN ISOLATIONIST ANALYSIS OF *WORLD WAR II!*

PATRICK J. BUCHANAN
A REPUBLIC NOT AN...

JOHN McCAIN AND DONALD TRUMP EACH RESPOND WITH BRAVE AND PRINCIPLED STATEMENTS *DE-NOUNCING* HITLER.

HE WAS *TOO* A BAD MAN!

VERY, VERY BAD!

(GEORGE W. BUSH, MEANWHILE, TRIES NOT TO ALIENATE THE NAZI VOTE.)

PLEASE DON'T LEAVE THE PARTY, PAT!

AND JUST TO KEEP THINGS *REALLY* STRANGE, BUCHAN-AN--IN AN ATTEMPT TO SECURE THE REFORM PARTY NOMINATION--FORGES AN ALLIANCE WITH LENORA FULANI, A SELF-DESCRIBED *MARXIST* AND *BLACK NATIONALIST.*

WE'VE ··REALLY GOT A LOT IN COMMON.

WE'RE *BOTH* CARBON-BASED LIFE ·· FORMS--AND *NEITHER* OF US CAN SURVIVE WITHOUT *OXYGEN!*

PAT BUCHANAN: THE WORLD'S FIRST *POLITICAL SUR-REALIST.*

MY FELLOW AMERICANS--I WOULD NOW LIKE TO SMEAR MY BODY WITH CHOCOLATE AND STRAWBERRIES AS I DENOUNCE THE SECRET MANIPULATIONS OF THE *INTERNATIONAL BANKERS!*

ISN'T HE SIMPLY *BRILLIANT* AT DECONSTRUCTING THE DARK UNDERCURRENTS OF IDEOLOG-ICAL EXTREMISM?

BRAVO, PAT, *BRAVO!*

UM--IT *IS* JUST A PER-FORMANCE-- RIGHT?

TOM TOMORROW©10-6-99... tomorrow@well.com ... www.thismodernworld.com

THIS MODERN WORLD

by TOM TOMORROW

THIS IS TRUE: IN HIS NEW, AUTHORIZED BIOGRAPHY OF RONALD REAGAN, EDMUND MORRIS EMPLOYS A BIZARRE LITERARY DEVICE -- THE INSERTION OF A FICTIONALIZED (AND MUCH OLDER) VERSION OF *HIMSELF* INTO REAGAN'S LIFE STORY...

SAY, EDMUND, BONZO AND I WERE WONDERING-- WHY ARE YOU ALWAYS SCRIBBLING IN THAT *NOTEBOOK?*

WELL, DUTCH... I JUST HAVE A FEELING THESE NOTES MIGHT COME IN HANDY SOME DAY...

TRADITIONAL HISTORIANS ARE APPALLED... BUT MAYBE THIS IS A FITTING TRIBUTE TO THE MAN WHOSE PRESIDENCY WAS *DEFINED* BY THE BLURRING OF FACT AND FICTION...

WELFARE MOTHERS ARE ALL DRIVING *CADILLACS!*

A BIG SPACE UMBRELLA WILL KEEP US ALL *SAFE FROM HARM!*

WE CAN CUT TAXES, INCREASE MILITARY SPENDING--*AND* BALANCE THE BUDGET!

WORD!

GOT THAT RIGHT!

YOU GO, GIRL!

OR MAYBE THIS IS A LONG-OVERDUE BREAKTHROUGH WHICH WILL HELP TO *POPULARIZE* HISTORICAL STUDIES... MAYBE MORE PEOPLE WOULD BE INTERESTED IN A BIOGRAPHY OF *RICHARD NIXON*, FOR INSTANCE, IF IT WERE TOLD FROM THE PERSPECTIVE OF HIS LIFELONG PAL *MARVIN*, THE MISCHEVIOUS *TALKING MOUSE*...

MARVIN, THERE ARE EIGHTEEN AND A HALF MINUTES OF TAPE MISSING! DO *YOU* KNOW ANYTHING ABOUT THIS?

ER--NO SIR, MR. PRESIDENT! *ULP!*

AND, FOR THAT MATTER, MAYBE THE DEFINITIVE *BILL CLINTON* BIOGRAPHY SHOULD BE TOLD FROM THE PERSPECTIVE OF--JUST TO CHOOSE AN EXAMPLE AT RANDOM--A *SMART-ASS PENGUIN*...

-- hiding under the desk, I watched Monica cavort salaciously in the pile of cash James Riady had just dropped off, as Bill laughed maniacally and declared, "This is what *I* call campaign finance reform!"

HEY! THAT NEVER HAPPENED!

YEAH, LIKE ANYBODY'S GONNA BELIEVE *YOU*...

TAP TAP TAP.

TOM TOMORROW ©9-29-99... tomorrow@well.com ... www.thismodernworld.com

THIS MODERN WORLD

by TOM TOMORROW

SO MAYBE THIS WILL BE A MARGINALLY INTERESTING PRIMARY SEASON AFTER ALL...YOU'VE GOT PAT BUCHANAN, JESSE VENTURA AND THE DONALD DUKING IT OUT IN THE *REFORM PARTY* SIDESHOW...

SHADY DELL
BISBEE, AZ

JOHN McCAIN IS MAKING NOISE ABOUT *CAMPAIGN FINANCE REFORM*...BILL BRADLEY IS STUMPING FOR *UNIVERSAL HEALTH COVERAGE*...HELL, WE MIGHT EVEN SEE WARREN BEATTY OUT THERE FLYING THE FLAG FOR GOOD OLD-FASHIONED *LIBERALISM!*

AND THEN, OF COURSE, GEORGE W. BUSH WILL BE ELECTED IN A LANDSLIDE.

ASSUMING THAT CIVILIZATION AS WE KNOW IT DOESN'T COLLAPSE TWO MONTHS FROM NOW.

READERS CAN ALWAYS COUNT ON US TO FIND THE CLOUD INSIDE THE SILVER LINING, EH, PERKINS?

IT'S OUR BEST THING.

THIS MODERN WORLD

by TOM TOMORROW

WE KNOW SOME OF YOU HAVE BEEN FEELING PRETTY SMUG SINCE THE KOSOVO CONFLICT.

WE DID WHAT HAD TO BE DONE, WITH NO THOUGHT FOR OURSELVES-- BECAUSE IT WAS THE *RIGHT THING TO DO.*

TRULY, WE ARE A *SELFLESS* AND *NOBLE* PEOPLE.

BUT RECENT EVENTS IN EAST TIMOR PROVIDE A DRAMATIC CONTRAST... AFTER ALL, THE U.S. HAS MORE THAN A LITTLE CULPABILITY *THERE*, HAVING SUPPLIED, TRAINED AND ARMED THE INDONESIAN MILITARY THROUGHOUT ITS ILLEGAL, QUARTER-CENTURY OCCUPATION OF THE TINY NATION...

WELL, YES-- BUT INDONESIA IS A STRATEGIC *ALLY!*

AND MANY U.S. CORPORATIONS HAVE PROFITABLE *INVESTMENTS* THERE!

WHAT'S A LITTLE INVASION BETWEEN *FRIENDS?*

HOWEVER... NOT ONLY DID WASHINGTON ALL BUT IGNORE THE RECENT MASSACRES-- IT TOOK A WEEK AND A HALF FOR THE CLINTON ADMINISTRATION TO EVEN SUSPEND *ARMS SALES* TO THE REGION.

BY GOD, IF THEY'RE GOING TO SLAUGHTER THE TIMORESE-- THEY'LL HAVE TO DO IT WITH WEAPONS WE'VE *ALREADY SOLD THEM!*

A BOLD AND DECISIVE MOVE, SIR!

ALL WE'RE SAYING IS, DON'T BREAK YOUR ARM PATTING YOURSELF ON THE BACK.

WELL-- WE DO THE RIGHT THING WHEN IT'S, UM, POLITICALLY *EXPEDIENT.*

AND U.S. BUSINESS INTERESTS ARE NOT AT STAKE.

WHAT MORE DO YOU *WANT?*

THIS MODERN WORLD

by TOM TOMORROW

FOR YEARS, CONSUMERS WERE HELD CAPTIVE BY THE GLASS-STEAGALL ACT.

HOW I WISH WE COULD BANK, INVEST IN THE STOCK MARKET, *AND* BUY LIFE INSURANCE--ALL UNDER *ONE ROOF!*

YES--IF ONLY WE DID NOT HAVE TO TRUDGE WEARILY FROM ONE LOCATION TO ANOTHER TO PERFORM SUCH TRANSACTIONS!

DAMN THESE RESTRICTIVE BANKING REGULATIONS! WHEN WILL THE MADNESS *END?*

FORTUNATELY, A SELFLESS ARMY OF LOBBYISTS HEEDED THEIR CALL!

SURE, WE MIGHT MAKE A FEW MILLION ON THIS-- BUT MORE *IMPORTANTLY,* WE'LL BE HELPING OUR FELLOW AMERICANS IN THEIR TIME OF *NEED!*

THE SYSTEM HAS GIVEN ENOUGH TO *US*--IT'S TIME TO GIVE SOMETHING *BACK!*

Fatton, Hoggs and Dough

DUBIOUS SENATORS WERE WON OVER IN SMOKY BACK ROOMS...

DON'T YOU SEE, PHIL--THE PEOPLE ARE *CRYING OUT* FOR ONE-STOP FINANCIAL SHOPPING!

WELL, IF YOU BOYS REALLY THINK IT'S IN THE BEST INTERESTS OF MY CONSTITUENTS-- WHAT CHOICE DO I *HAVE?*

I'M ONLY HERE AS THEIR HUMBLE SERVANT, AFTER ALL!

AND AT LONG LAST, THE BANKING INDUSTRY WAS FREED FROM THE ANTIQUATED SHACKLES OF GOVERNMENTAL OVERSIGHT!

TO THINK THAT THEY WENT TO SO MUCH TROUBLE--JUST TO MAKE *OUR* LIVES *EASIER!*

WHO *SAYS* POLITICIANS NEVER DO ANYTHING FOR THE LITTLE GUY?

NOW IF THEY'D JUST ELIMINATE ALL THOSE DAMNED *FOOD SAFETY REGULATIONS*--WE'D BE LIVING IN A VERITABLE *PARADISE!*

REMEMBER, CITIZENS--WHAT'S GOOD FOR *BUSINESS* IS GOOD FOR *YOU!*

TOM TOMORROW©11-3-99... tomorrow@well.com ... www.thismodernworld.com

THIS MODERN WORLD

by TOM TOMORROW

GREAT NEWS, EVERYONE! ACCORDING TO THE NEW YORK TIMES, INVESTORS INCLUDING *MICHAEL MILKEN* ARE HOPING TO TRANSFORM THE *EDUCATIONAL SYSTEM* INTO "THE NEXT HEALTH CARE!"

WELL, IT CERTAINLY MAKES SENSE-- GIVEN THE UNMITIGATED SUCCESS OF THE *H.M.O.* INDUSTRY!

AND IF YOU CAN'T TRUST *MICHAEL MILKEN* WITH YOUR CHILDREN'S FUTURE--

--WHO *CAN* YOU TRUST?

WHY, JUST *IMAGINE* THE SAVINGS THAT WILL ENSUE WHEN COST-EFFECTIVE, H.M.O.-STYLE MANAGEMENT TECHNIQUES ARE APPLIED TO OUR NATION'S *SCHOOLS!*

AH, MS. PERIWINKLE, WE AT MILKEN LEARNING INDUSTRIES HAVE DETERMINED THAT THE YEARS 1861 THROUGH 1914 ARE NOT EDUCATIONALLY *NECESSARY*--SO LET'S HURRY THE CLASS ALONG TO THE FIRST WORLD WAR, SHALL WE?

GRRRR

TODAY'S LESSON: THE INDUSTRIAL REVOLUTION

AFTER ALL, ISN'T IT ABOUT *TIME* SOMEONE BROUGHT A LITTLE FREE MARKET *DISCIPLINE* TO THE SOCIALISTIC ENTITLEMENT PROGRAM KNOWN AS *PUBLIC EDUCATION?*

BILLY, YOUR PARENTS HAVEN'T KEPT UP WITH THEIR PREMIUMS--SO BEFORE MR. CONWAY EXPLAINS THE ISOSCELES TRIANGLE, I'M AFRAID I'LL HAVE TO ASK YOU TO LEAVE THE ROOM.

HA, HA!

AND WITH WATCHFUL SHAREHOLD[ERS] AWAITING A RETURN ON THEIR [...] YOU CAN JUST *BET* THAT THE[SE] SCHOOLS WILL GET A *GOLD ST[AR]*

CONGRATULATIONS, SON! [...] YOUR *HIGH SCHOOL DI[PLOMA]* RUN ALONG NOW!

GRADUATION CLASS OF NOV., 2002

?

THIS MODERN WORLD

by TOM TOMORROW

SOME PEOPLE THINK THERE'S TOO MUCH *CYNICISM* IN PUBLIC DISCOURSE THESE DAYS... SO IN THE INTEREST *OF FAIRNESS*, LET'S TAKE THE FOLLOWING *ACTUAL QUOTE* FROM THE PRESIDENT AT *FACE VALUE*...

"SINCE I SIGNED THE TELECOMMUNICATIONS BILL, OVER 300,000 NEW HIGH-TECH JOBS HAVE BEEN CREATED... OVER 20,000 AMERICANS ARE NOW MAKING A LIVING DOING BUSINESS ON EBAY... INCLUDING A SUBSTANTIAL NUMBER OF *FORMER WELFARE RECIPIENTS!*"

NOW, GIVEN THE RELATIVE ANONYMITY OF EBAY'S REGISTRATION PROCESS, A *CYNIC* MIGHT WONDER HOW THE PRESIDENT COULD POSSIBLY *KNOW* THIS-- BUT NOT *US!*

WE FIGURE THERE MUST BE A SECRET GOVERNMENT AGENCY TRACKING THE ONLINE ACTIVITY OF *EVERY AMERICAN* -- AND THEN CROSS-CHECKING THE INFORMATION AGAINST AN ALL-INCLUSIVE *WELFARE RECIPIENT DATABASE!*

WE'VE GOT A POSITIVE MATCH IN SECTOR 14, SIR!

GOOD WORK, JENKINS! I'D BETTER GET THIS TO THE PRESIDENT *IMMEDIATELY!*

NOR WOULD IT EVER *OCCUR* TO US TO ASK HOW THESE PRESUMABLY IMPOVERISHED WELFARE RECIPIENTS MANAGED TO SCRAPE TOGETHER THE MONEY FOR A COMPUTER, SCANNER AND INTERNET CONNECTION TO GET THEIR EBAY BUSINESSES *STARTED*...

I FOUND SOME MORE CHANGE UNDER THE CUSHIONS, MA!

THANKS, HONEY! ONLY $847.30 MORE TO *GO!*

AS LONG AS WE DON'T SPEND ANY MONEY ON FOOD OR RENT.

AND WE'RE *CLEARLY* FAR TOO EARNEST AND IDEALISTIC TO WONDER -- WELL -- EXACTLY *WHAT* SOUGHT-AFTER ITEMS THEY FOUND TO *SELL* IN SUCH VAST QUANTITIES THAT THEY ARE NOW ABLE TO SUPPORT THEMSELVES THROUGH THEIR ONLINE AUCTIONS *ALONE*...

LOOK AT THAT, EARL! I GOT TWELVE DOLLARS FOR THE *KITCHEN TABLE* -- THREE DOLLARS FOR THE *CAT* -- AND A BUCK FIFTY FOR THE BOY'S *UNDERPANTS!*

I WONDER HOW MUCH THE *FLOORBOARDS* ARE WORTH!

I'LL GO GET A *CROWBAR.*

THAT'S THE SPIRIT, FOLKS! WHO NEEDS A SOCIAL SAFETY NET -- WHEN WE'VE GOT THE *INTERNET?*

NEXT WEEK: WE TAKE THE *TOOTH FAIRY* AT *FACE VALUE!*

TOM TOMORROW © 11-24-99 ... TIP O' THE PEN (GUIN) TO JOSH MASON!

THIS SENSATIONAL WORLD

TOM TOMORROW ANSWERS **YOUR** QUESTIONS ABOUT THE BROOKLYN MUSEUM OF ART'S "SENSATION" SHOW!

1) HOW DOES ANYONE KNOW CHRIS OFILI'S HIGHLY STYLIZED PAINTING IS MEANT TO REPRESENT THE HOLY VIRGIN MARY?

BECAUSE IT IS TITLED "THE HOLY VIRGIN MARY." IF HE'D CALLED IT "MADELINE ALBRIGHT," NO ONE WOULD HAVE GIVEN IT A SECOND THOUGHT.

IT DOESN'T **LOOK** LIKE MADELINE ALBRIGHT.

WELL, WHO DO **YOU** THINK IT IS -- THE **VIRGIN MOTHER?**

OF COURSE, THEN WE WOULD HAVE NEVER HEARD RUDY GIULIANI SETTLE (BY A PROCESS OF ELIMINATION) THE AGE-OLD QUESTION OF WHAT **ART** REALLY **IS**...

IF **I** CAN DO IT --

-- IT'S **NOT** ART!

MEN

2) ARE THE CRITICS OF THIS SHOW JUST A BUNCH OF YAHOOS WHO WOULD FEEL MORE AT HOME IN, SAY, OKLAHOMA?

PROBABLY... BUT LET'S BE HONEST -- THE ARTISTS WHO CLAIM TO BE SHOCKED, **SHOCKED** THAT THEIR WORK COULD STIR UP SUCH CONTROVERSY **ARE** BEING JUST A WEE BIT **DISINGENUOUS**...

WHEN I PAINTED "FUCKING JESUS UP THE ASS WITH A TWELVE-INCH DILDO" --

-- I HAD NO **IDEA** PEOPLE WOULD GET SO UPSET!

AFTER ALL, ONE OF THE MOST TEDIOUS THINGS ABOUT THESE PERIODIC BATTLES IS THAT FREE SPEECH ADVOCATES ARE REPEATEDLY FORCED TO DEFEND THE ARTISTIC MERITS OF BANAL, SHOCK-VALUE **SCATOLOGY**...

YOU SEE, THE CRUCIFIX DIPPED IN URINE IS A **POWERFUL STATEMENT** --

-- ABOUT, UM, **CRUCIFIXES**.

AND **URINE!**

AND...IT SHOULD ALSO BE NOTED THAT EVEN IN THE *ART* WORLD, SOME WONDER IF THIS EXHIBITION IS JUST A CYNICAL PLOY TO DRIVE UP THE VALUE OF CHARLES SAATCHI'S *INVESTMENTS*...

SURE, THE JONESES HAVE A *MATISSE* -- BUT WE HAVE DAMIEN HIRST'S ROTTING COW HEAD SURROUNDED BY LIVE FLIES AND MAGGOTS!

IT LOOKS *MARVELOUS* IN OUR *FOYER!*

3) IF THE SHOW IS ADMITTEDLY CONTROVERSIAL, WHY SHOULD TAXPAYERS WHO ARE OFFENDED BY IT BE FORCED TO *FUND* IT?

GOSH--WHAT A *GOOD POINT!* LIKE THE I.R.S. ALWAYS SAYS, IF YOU'RE NOT HAPPY WITH THE WAY YOUR TAX DOLLARS ARE BEING SPENT-- THEN YOU DESERVE A *REFUND!*

INTERNAL REVENUE SERVI
"Satisfactio..Guaranteed!"

YOUR PORTION OF THE EXHIBITION COMES TO 1/50TH OF A PENNY.

PLEASE FILL OUT THESE FORMS IN TRIPLICATE AND WE'LL SEND YOU A CHECK.

HECK--UNLESS YOU BELIEVE THAT MUSEUMS HAVE SOME SORT OF "MISSION" TO SERVE AS THE CULTURAL "REPOSITORIES" OF OUR "SOCIETY"-- MAYBE IT *WOULD* BE BEST IF THE MAYOR PROCEEDED WITH HIS PLAN TO *EVICT* THE MUSEUM AS QUICKLY AS *POSSIBLE*--

AND DON'T FORGET TO CLEAR THAT *EGYPTIAN* GARBAGE OUT, TOO!

GRRRR

STARBUCKS WANTS TO TAKE THE BUILDING OVER BY *FRIDAY!*

--AND *THEN*, WE CAN ALL STRIVE FOR A WORLD IN WHICH ART IS SIMPLY NOT ALLOWED IN PUBLICLY-FUNDED SPACES--UNLESS IT IS GUARANTEED TO UPSET *NO ONE*...

MOMMY, THAT PUPPY IS MAKING ME *SAD!*

WELL, LET'S TELL THE MAYOR, HONEY--AND HE CAN CLOSE THIS PLACE *DOWN!*

"The artist does not create for the artist, he creates for the people, and we will see to it that henceforth the people will be called in to judge its art." --Adolf Hitler

(ORIGINALLY APPEARED IN THE *VILLAGE VOICE*.)

THIS MODERN WORLD

by TOM TOMORROW

Panel 1:

WELCOME TO "*WHO WANTS TO BE A BILLIONAIRE!*" OUR FIRST CONTESTANT IS ONE OF THE THREE FACELESS BUREAUCRATS WHO SIT ON THE WORLD TRADE ORGANIZATION'S *RULING TRIBUNAL* -- WEARING A DISGUISE TO PRESERVE HIS *ANONYMITY*, OF COURSE!

LET'S GET STARTED, ANONYMOUS BUREAUCRAT! FOR $100, WERE THE PROTESTERS IN SEATTLE --

Panel 2:

-- (A) A BUNCH OF KNOW-NOTHING, ANTI-CAPITALIST SUBVERSIVES WHO PROVE THE NEED FOR A NEW SEDITION ACT --

-- OR (B) AMERICAN CITIZENS CONCERNED ABOUT THE ANTI-DEMOCRATIC EFFECTS OF A SECRETIVE GLOBAL BODY EMPOWERED TO OVERRULE ANY NATION'S LAWS IN THE NAME OF FREE TRADE?

WELL, BILL -- THE ANSWER IS CLEARLY (A)!

FINAL ANSWER?

Panel 3:

YES, FINAL ANSWER. BUT BEFORE WE GO ANY FURTHER, I'M GOING TO HAVE TO ASK YOU TO DECLARE ME THE *WINNER* AND GIVE ME THE BILLION DOLLARS.

UM -- THAT'S NOT REALLY HOW THE RULES OF THE GAME ARE SET UP --

Panel 4:

THE W.T.O. DOESN'T CARE ABOUT YOUR LITTLE RULES! THE W.T.O. MAKES ITS *OWN* RULES -- AND THEY'RE *NOT* SUBJECT TO APPEAL! YOU KNOW THAT, YOU SCHMUCK -- YOU SIGNED THE TREATY!

NOW HAND OVER THE DAMN CHECK -- OR FACE HARSH SANCTIONS FOR EXPROPRIATING MY POTENTIAL *PROFITS*!

Panel 5:

Panel 6:

WELL, FOLKS -- IT LOOKS LIKE WE'VE GOT A *WINNER!* TUNE IN NEXT TIME -- WHEN OUR CONTESTANT WILL BE *RALPH NADER!*

I'VE GOT A FEELING *HE'LL* FIND OUR GAME A LITTLE MORE ... *CHALLENGING...*

PAY TO THE ORDER OF: ANONYMOUS BUREAUCRAT ONE BILLION DOLLARS!
Bill Clinton

TOM TOMORROW ©12-8-99 ... tomorrow@well.com ... www.thismodernworld.com

90

THIS MODERN WORLD

by TOM TOMORROW

IF NOT FOR THE SEATTLE PROTESTS, DISCUSSION OF THE WORLD TRADE ORGANIZATION WOULD HAVE REMAINED AT A NEAR-KINDERGARTEN LEVEL.

FREE TRADE BENEFITS *EVERYONE*, BOYS AND GIRLS! ANYONE WHO DOESN'T UNDERSTAND *THAT* IS A *BIG SILLY-HEAD!*

CAN *YOU* SAY "BIG SILLY-HEAD"?

I KNEW YOU COULD!

OF COURSE, THERE *IS* A BIT MORE TO THE STORY... I.E., THE PROFOUNDLY ANTI-DEMOCRATIC NATURE OF THE W.T.O., WHOSE SECRETIVE THREE-MEMBER TRIBUNAL IS EMPOWERED TO OVERRULE THE LAWS OF ANY MEMBER NATION IN THE NAME OF *FREE TRADE*...

I DON'T SEE ANY PROBLEM WITH THAT.

I DON'T HEAR ANYONE COMPLAINING.

I HAVE NO COMMENT.

World Trade Organization

...WHICH BRINGS US TO THE HEART OF THE PROBLEM: THE GROWING DOMINANCE OF AN ECONOMIC SYSTEM IN WHICH GOVERNMENTS PLACE THE NEEDS OF LARGE CORPORATIONS OVER THOSE OF THEIR *OWN CITIZENRY*...

--A SYSTEM THE ITALIANS LONG AGO TERMED "ESTATO CORPORATIVO"--

--OR, MORE POPULARLY, "*FASCISM*."

YOU'RE MAKING ONE OF YOUR LITTLE POINTS AGAIN, AREN'T YOU?

IF ONLY THERE WERE SOME WAY TO COUNTER THIS TREND.

YES--IF ONLY WE HAD A SYSTEM IN WHICH EVERY CITIZEN HAD AN *EQUAL* VOICE-- *REGARDLESS* OF THEIR SOCIAL OR ECONOMIC STATUS!

AND SOME METHOD FOR-- WELL--*TALLYING* THEIR BELIEFS, SO THAT THE WILL OF THE *MAJORITY* COULD SOMEHOW BE IMPLEMENTED!

WELL-- I SURE CAN'T THINK OF ANYTHING LIKE *THAT!*

THIS MODERN WORLD

by TOM TOMORROW

THEY SMILE REASSURINGLY AND TELL YOU EVERYTHING'S FINE, THAT THE ECONOMY'S GOING GANG-BUSTERS AND A RISING TIDE LIFTS ALL BOATS--BUT YOU KNOW THAT SOMETHING'S WRONG HERE. YOU KNOW THAT 85% OF THE WEALTH IS CONTROLLED BY 20% OF THE POPULATION... THAT THE WAGES OF A MAJORITY OF AMERICANS ARE ACTUALLY LOWER, IN REAL DOL-LARS, THAN THEY WERE IN *1973*.

YOU KNOW THAT YOUR LEADERS HAVE BEEN BOUGHT AND PAID FOR, THAT CORPORATE MONEY SETS THE POLITICAL AGENDA. YOU KNOW THAT THE FREE MAR-KET HAS BECOME THE DOMINANT RELIGION OF OUR AGE... THAT ANYONE FOOLISH ENOUGH TO SUGGEST TEMPERING THE QUEST FOR PROFIT WITH A MODICUM OF CONCERN FOR HUMAN RIGHTS OR THE ENVIRONMENT IS VIEWED AS A HERETIC--IF NOT AN UTTER LUNATIC.

YOU KNOW THAT SOMETHING IS DEEPLY, FUNDAMENTALLY WRONG.

BUT WHAT CAN YOU DO? YOU DON'T MATTER. YOUR VOTE DOESN'T MATTER. YOUR PROTESTS DON'T MAT-TER. GO AHEAD, MARCH IN THE STREETS AND CHANT YOUR LITTLE SLOGANS. THE POLITICAL SOPHIS-TICATES AND MEDIA ELITES WILL SMIRK AT YOUR NAIVETÉ, YOUR MISGUIDED NOSTALGIA FOR THE SIXTIES, AND THEN THEY WILL STEER THE CONVERSATION BACK TO THE STOCK MARKET. OR THE FABULOUS NEW RESTAURANT THEY'VE RECENTLY DISCOVERED. THEY'RE NOT WORRIED ABOUT YOU.

AND YET... SOMETHING EXTRAOR-DINARY JUST HAPPENED IN SEATTLE. DEMONSTRATORS TOOK TO THE STREETS AND MADE THEIR VOICES HEARD--AND IT *MADE A DIFFERENCE*. THE MEDIA WERE FORCED TO ADDRESS ISSUES THEY HAD PREVIOUSLY SWEPT UNDER THE RUG, TO EX-PLAIN WHY ANYONE COULD POSSIBLY BE OPPOSED TO UN-FETTERED GLOBAL CAPITALISM. IN A FEW SHORT DAYS, THE ENTIRE DEBATE WAS ALTERED, PERHAPS IRREVOCABLY.

YOU KNOW SOMETHING'S WRONG. MAYBE IT'S TIME TO START MAK-ING SOME NOISE ABOUT IT.

HAPPY NEW MILLENNIUM.

TOM TOMORROW©12-22-99... tomorrow@well.com ... www.thismodernworld.com

92

THIS MODERN WORLD

by TOM TOMORROW

Panel 1: THE END OF THE MILLENNIUM HAD FINALLY ARRIVED.

SAYS HERE THAT BILL GATES PRETTY MUCH OWNS EVERYTHING.

THAT'S NICE. WILL YOU PLEASE PASS THE SUGAR?

Panel 2: AT THE STROKE OF MIDNIGHT, DEC. 31, 1999, COMPUTERS EVERYWHERE SET THEMSELVES BACK AN ENTIRE CENTURY--

Panel 3: --AND UNEXPECTEDLY TOOK ALL OF SOCIETY BACK *WITH* THEM.

Panel 4: AMERICANS FOUND THEMSELVES THRUST INTO A TIME IN WHICH VAST WEALTH AND RESOURCES WERE CONCENTRATED IN THE HANDS OF A VERY *FEW*--

Panel 5: --WHILE THE MOST BASIC NEEDS OF THE INDIGENT AND THE WORKING POOR WERE ALL BUT *IGNORED.*

Panel 6: OBVIOUSLY, EVERYONE FELT RIGHT AT HOME.

SAYS HERE THAT JOHN D. ROCKEFELLER PRETTY MUCH OWNS *EVERYTHING.*

THAT'S NICE. WILL YOU PLEASE PASS THE SUGAR?

TOM TOMORROW ©12-30-98

THIS MODERN WORLD

by TOM TOMORROW

SO, SPARKY--THE END OF THE MILLENNIUM IS JUST *MOMENTS* AWAY! ARE YOU *SURE* YOU'RE NOT WORRIED ABOUT Y2K BREAKDOWNS?

HAPPY NEW YEAR!

11:57

LET'S JUST SAY I'M RESIGNED TO A CERTAIN DEGREE OF INCONVENIENCE...I MEAN, *SOME* AMOUNT OF DATA WILL INEVITABLY GET SCRAMBLED SOMEWHERE--AT THE BANK, MAYBE, OR THE PHONE COMPANY--

HAPPY NEW YEAR!

11:58

--MAYBE EVEN AT THE NEWSPAPERS THAT RUN OUR CARTOON...BUT EVEN IF THAT HAPPENS--HOW BAD CAN IT REALLY *BE*?

11:59

12:00

ADMITTEDLY, I WOULDN'T HAVE ANTICIPATED *THIS*.

LOVE *IS*...FACING UNEXPECTED OBSTACLES *TOGETHER*!

OH, SHUT THE HELL UP.

12:01

94

THIS MODERN WORLD

by TOM TOMORROW

Panel 1: I HAD THE STRANGEST DREAM THE OTHER NIGHT... GEORGE W. BUSH SAID THAT THE POLITICAL PHILOSOPHER WHO'D MOST INFLUENCED HIM WAS *ODIN*...

YES, THAT'S RIGHT -- THE NORSE GOD OF WISDOM AND VICTORY! I TURNED MY LIFE OVER TO HIM AND IT CHANGED MY HEART!

YOU GOT A *PROBLEM* WITH THAT?

Panel 2: GARY BAUER AND STEVE FORBES KEPT TALKING ABOUT THEIR DEEP AND ABIDING FAITH IN THE *UNARIAN SPACE BROTHERS*...

THEY'LL ARRIVE SOON, YOU KNOW--FROM PLANETS AS DIVERSE AS ZETON, SEVERUS, KALLIUM AND BRUNDAGE!

YES--JUST AS IT WAS FORETOLD BY THE INFALLIBLE ARCHANGEL URIEL!

IT'S A FACT!

WELCOME

Panel 3: ...AND AL GORE WANTED EVERYONE TO KNOW THAT HE OFTEN TURNS TO THE SPIRIT OF *ELVIS* FOR SOLACE AND INSPIRATION!

THE KING SAYS I SHOULD EAT A PEANUT BUTTER AND BANANA SANDWICH AND SHOOT SOME DAMN TV SCREENS ALL TO HELL.

ER--I'M NOT QUITE SURE HOW THAT APPLIES TO OUR CAMPAIGN STRATEGY, SIR.

GORE 2000

Panel 4: FORTUNATELY, IT WAS JUST A *CRAZY DREAM.*

BOY, WAS IT *EVER!*

YEAH, I MEAN -- COME *ON--*

--WHO EVER HEARD OF A *NON-CHRISTIAN PRESIDENTIAL CANDIDATE?!*

HA, HA

HA, HA

TOM TOMORROW ©1-12-00...tomorrow@well.com ... www.thismodernworld.com

THIS MODERN WORLD

by TOM TOMORROW

NEXT ON THE AOL-TIME WARNER NETWORK--IT'S *LARRY KING LIVE!*

GOOD EVENING! MY GUESTS TONIGHT ARE STEVE CASE OF AOL AND GERALD LEVIN OF TIME WARNER! I UNDERSTAND YOU GENTLEMEN HAVE AN *ANNOUNCEMENT* FOR US!

THAT'S *RIGHT,* LARRY! AS PART OF THE AOL-TIME WARNER MERGER--

--GERALD AND I HAVE DECIDED TO HAVE BOTH OUR HEADS GRAFTED ONTO A *SINGLE BODY!*

YOU SEE, LARRY, WE FELT THE WORLD'S LARGEST INTERNET-NEWS-AND-ENTERTAINMENT CONGLOMERATE SHOULD HAVE A *SINGLE CHIEF EXECUTIVE OFFICER!*

WE'LL SAVE TIME SLEEPING, EATING, AND TAKING CARE OF OTHER ROUTINE BODILY FUNCTIONS--AND WE'LL PASS THE BENEFITS ALONG TO OUR *SHAREHOLDERS!*

THAT'S *GREAT,* GUYS! SO--DO YOU HAVE ANY PLANS FOR *FURTHER EXPANSION?*

WELL, WE CAN'T REALLY TALK ABOUT THAT RIGHT NOW, LARRY--

HA, HA!

--BUT LET'S JUST SAY WE'VE STILL GOT PLENTY OF ROOM FOR *BILL GATES'* HEAD! HA, HA!

TOM TOMORROW© 1-19-00 ... tomorrow@well.com ... www.thismodernworld.com

THIS MODERN WORLD

by TOM TOMORROW

HAVE YOU *HEARD*, BIFF? AMERICA ONLINE AND TIME WARNER ARE *MERGING*!

YOU MEAN THE WORLD'S LARGEST PROVIDER OF INTERNET ACCESS IS JOINING FORCES WITH THE WORLD'S LARGEST MEDIA CONGLOMERATE? WHY, THAT'S *TERRIFIC*!

JUST *IMAGINE* THE BENEFITS FOR CONSUMERS SUCH AS OURSELVES! A.O.L. WILL BE ABLE TO LINK TO TIME MAGAZINE COVER STORIES HYPING WARNER BROTHERS MOVIES--

--AND LARRY KING CAN INTERVIEW *EVERYONE INVOLVED*!

THE WORLD IS ONE STEP CLOSER TO A *SINGLE SOURCE* OF NEWS, INFORMATION AND ENTERTAINMENT!

I ALWAYS FOUND ALL THOSE DIFFERENT COMPANY NAMES *TERRIBLY* CONFUSING!

OH, BIFF--WOULDN'T IT BE WONDERFUL IF A.O.L. TIME WARNER MERGED WITH *MICROSOFT*?

YOU'RE A CRAZY DREAMER, WANDA-- BUT THAT'S WHY I LOVE YOU!

©TOM TOMORROW

THIS MODERN WORLD

by TOM TOMORROW

THIS WEEK: A PEEK BEHIND THE SCENES AT _THIS MODERN WORLD!_

WE'RE HERE PREPARING FOR OUR NEXT CARTOON...YOU ALL KNOW BIFF, OF COURSE--HE'S OUR BUFFOONISH CARICATURE OF CONSERVATIVE THOUGHT, OUR RESIDENT _STRAW MAN_...

GOT THIS WEEK'S LINES MEMORIZED YET, BIFF?

AHEM! "SPARKY, I DON'T SEE WHAT'S WRONG WITH TEACHING CHRISTIAN CREATION MYTHS IN LIEU OF _ACTUAL SCIENCE!_"

GREAT WORK, BIFF! SEE YOU ON THE SET!

IN REAL LIFE, BIFF SPENDS MOST EVENINGS STUDYING THE WORK OF _NOAM CHOMSKY!_

HERE IN THE MAKEUP DEPARTMENT IS _FRANK WILLIAMS_--THE ACTOR WHO PLAYS _BILL CLINTON_ FOR US!

HI FOLKS! PERSONALLY, I THINK THIS CARTOON IS TOO HARD ON CLINTON--BUT HEY, IT'S BEEN STEADY WORK! AND I'M NOT GOING TO HAVE MUCH OF THAT _NEXT_ YEAR!

DON'T WORRY, FRANK --WE'LL STILL BRING YOU BACK FOR THE OCCASIONAL _RETROSPECTIVE!_

NOW, AS YOU PROBABLY KNOW, I PLAY THE KNOW-IT-ALL PENGUIN WHO ALWAYS GETS THE FINAL WORD! HEH--IF ONLY REAL LIFE WERE LIKE THAT! OF COURSE, HERE ON THE SET, I'VE GOT THE BENEFIT OF A BLATANTLY BIASED, _PRE-SCRIPTED ENCOUNTER_...

...WHICH BRINGS US TO OUR FINAL STOP...AFTER ALL, WE CERTAINLY CAN'T CONCLUDE OUR LITTLE PEEK BEHIND THE CURTAIN WITHOUT DROPPING IN ON _TOM TOMORROW_--WHO SPENDS MOST OF _HIS_ TIME ALONE IN THIS _LITTLE ROOM_, STARING AT HIS _COMPUTER SCREEN_--

GO AWAY!

DO NOT DISTURB

--TRYING TO THINK OF NEW WAYS TO EXPRESS HIS DEEP-ROOTED CONVICTION THAT HE'S SMARTER THAN _EVERYONE ELSE_...

MUTTER, MUTTER... WHY DON'T THEY LISTEN TO ME? I'LL SHOW THEM! I'LL SHOW THEM _ALL!_ MUTTER MUTTER...

KIND OF CREEPY WHEN YOU THINK ABOUT IT--BUT HEY-- IT KEEPS HIM OFF THE _STREETS!_

SEE YOU NEXT WEEK, FOLKS!

TOM TOMORROW ©01-05-00... tomorrow@well.com ... www.thismodernworld.com

THIS MODERN WORLD

by TOM TOMORROW

THE THING THAT STRIKES A VISITOR TO THE SOUTH IS THE EXTENT TO WHICH IT IS STILL DEFINED BY THE **CIVIL WAR**...MEMORIALS AND MONUMENTS DOT THE LANDSCAPE, AND EVERYWHERE YOU LOOK THERE ARE EXPRESSIONS OF SOUTHERN PRIDE ACCOMPANIED BY REPRESENTATIONS OF THE **CONFEDERATE FLAG**...

(ACTUAL SOUVENIRS FROM A RECENT ROAD TRIP)

I HAVE A DREAM WASHINGTON DC © THE FUTURE CO.

If I Had Known This **I WOULD HAVE PICKED MY OWN COTTON**

FORGET, HELL!

IN SOUTH CAROLINA, THAT FLAG WAS RAISED ABOVE THE STATE CAPITAL IN 1962, AS A SUPPOSEDLY **TEMPORARY** COMMEMORATION OF THE CENTENNIAL OF THE CIVIL WAR...THOUGH SOMEHOW THEY FORGOT TO EVER TAKE IT **DOWN**...

MUST HAVE SLIPPED OUR MINDS--WHAT WITH ALL THOSE CIVIL RIGHTS MARCHES AND SEGREGATION BATTLES GOING ON!

HA, HA! JUST CALL US **ABSENT MINDED!**

NOW, MANY WHO SUPPORT THE FLAG'S CONTINUED DISPLAY ARE UNDOUBTEDLY SINCERE IN THEIR DESIRE TO CELEBRATE **CERTAIN** ASPECTS OF THEIR HERITAGE WHILE OVERLOOKING **OTHERS**-- THOUGH YOU'D THINK THE COGNITIVE DISSONANCE OF THE EFFORT WOULD MAKE THEIR **HEADS EXPLODE**...

IT'S NOT ABOUT RACISM--IT'S ABOUT TRADITION--**WHOOPS!**

WE JUST WANT TO HONOR THE SOUTHERN WAY OF LIFE--**AAACK!**

URRK!

YEAAGH!

BUT UNFORTUNATELY, THE STARS AND BARS SYMBOLIZE A SHAMEFUL PAST AS SURELY AS THE GERMAN **SWASTIKA**...THOUGH OF COURSE NOT EVERYONE IS WILLING TO **ACKNOWLEDGE** THIS...

GOVERNOR, HOW DO YOU FEEL ABOUT **CROSS BURNINGS** AND **LYNCHINGS**?

WHATEVER THE PEOPLE OF SOUTH CAROLINA DECIDE TO DO IS THEIR **OWN BUSINESS!**

AND THAT'S ALL I'M GOING TO SAY.

TOM TOMORROW ©1-26-00 ... tomorrow@well.com ... www.thismodernworld.com

99

THIS MODERN WORLD

by TOM TOMORROW

WHILE VISITING NEW YORK, BETSY CONSALLIS OF FAYETTEVILLE, ARKANSAS GETS LOST ON THE SUBWAY SYSTEM AND IS NEVER SEEN AGAIN--LEAVING HER SIX YEAR OLD SON ALLEN IN THE CARE OF *RELATIVES*...

--AND WE'VE DECIDED TO *KEEP* THE BOY!

AFTER ALL, NEW YORK HAS *MUCH* MORE TO OFFER HIM THAN *ARKANSAS*! I MEAN, GET *REAL*!

?

ALLEN'S FATHER, SPEAKING THROUGH AN INTERPRETER, MAKES A PASSIONATE PLEA FOR THE BOY'S RETURN TO ARKANSAS.

AH'M ORN'RIER THAN A RAZORBACK HAWG WITH A STICK UP HIS BEE-HIND! AH MAHT JEST COME UP THERE TO NEW YORK WITH MAH THIRTY-AUGHT-SIX, AH TELL YEW WHUT!

MR. CONSALLIS IS USING A COLORFUL METAPHOR TO EXPRESS HIS FRUSTRATION, AND SUGGESTS HE MIGHT TRAVEL TO NEW YORK WITH--UM--I BELIEVE IT'S SOME SORT OF FIREARM.

THE LITTLE BOY'S PLIGHT QUICKLY BECOMES THE *TALK* OF THE *TOWN!*

WELL, I SUPPOSE A BOY *SHOULD* BE WITH HIS FATHER--

--BUT NOW THAT HE'S TASTED *SOPHISTICATION*, CAN WE REALLY CONDEMN HIM TO A LIFE IN *ARKANSAS*?

I DON'T THINK THEY EVEN HAVE *MUSEUMS* THERE!

THE TUG OF WAR OVER LITTLE ALLEN'S FUTURE CONTINUES--BUT MEANWHILE, HE'S LIVING THE LIFE OF AN *AVERAGE NEW YORK CITY YOUNGSTER!*

LOOK, ALLEN! RUDY GIULIANI AND MICKEY MOUSE ARE HERE TO GIVE YOU A GUIDED TOUR OF THE *DISNEY STORE!*

YOU CAN HAVE *ANYTHING* IN THERE YOU WANT--*FREE!*

SO--DO YOU *REALLY* WANT TO GO BACK TO ARKANSAS?

UM--AON'T KNOW...

THIS MODERN WORLD

by TOM TOMORROW

THAT BOYISHLY TOUSLED HAIR.

THOSE ADORABLE JUG EARS.

THAT DEVIL-MAY-CARE GRIN.

DOESN'T THIS GUY SEEM VAGUELY...*FAMILIAR*?

WHAT--ME WORRY?

THIS MODERN WORLD

by TOM TOMORROW and RICHARD NIXON

THIS WEEK: MORE WISDOM FROM THE LATE, REVERED

RICHARD MILHOUS NIXON!

ACTUAL EXCERPTS FROM THE LATEST NIXON WHITE HOUSE TAPES RELEASED BY THE NATIONAL ARCHIVES!*

*TRANSCRIBED BY JAMES WARREN, CHICAGO TRIBUNE (AS REPRINTED IN HARPER'S)

WE'RE GOING TO (PUT) MORE OF THESE LITTLE NEGRO BASTARDS ON THE WELFARE ROLLS AT $2,400 A FAMILY... WORK, WORK. THROW 'EM OFF THE ROLLS. THAT'S THE KEY... I HAVE THE GREATEST AFFECTION FOR THEM, BUT I KNOW THEY'RE NOT GOING TO MAKE IT FOR 500 YEARS. THEY AREN'T. YOU KNOW IT, TOO.

THE MEXICANS ARE A DIFFERENT CUP OF TEA. THEY HAVE A HERITAGE. AT THE PRESENT TIME THEY STEAL, THEY'RE DISHONEST, BUT THEY DO HAVE SOME CONCEPT OF FAMILY LIFE. THEY DON'T LIVE LIKE A BUNCH OF DOGS, WHICH THE NEGROES DO LIVE LIKE.

YOU KNOW WHAT HAPPENED TO THE ROMANS? THE LAST SIX ROMAN EMPERORS WERE FAGS... YOU KNOW WHAT HAPPENED TO THE POPES? THEY WERE LAYIN' THE NUNS, THAT'S BEEN GOIN' ON FOR YEARS, CENTURIES. BUT THE CATHOLIC CHURCH WENT TO HELL THREE OR FOUR CENTURIES AGO. IT WAS HOMOSEXUAL AND IT HAD TO BE CLEANED OUT.

LOOK AT THE STRONG SOCIETIES. THE RUSSIANS. GODDAMN, THEY ROOT 'EM OUT. THEY DON'T LET 'EM AROUND AT ALL. I DON'T KNOW WHAT THEY DO WITH THEM. LOOK AT THIS COUNTRY. YOU THINK THE RUSSIANS ALLOW DOPE? HOMOSEXUALITY, DOPE, IMMORALITY ARE THE ENEMIES OF STRONG SOCIETIES.

THE UPPER CLASS OF SAN FRANCISCO IS THAT WAY. THE BOHEMIAN GROVE, WHICH I ATTEND FROM TIME TO TIME--IT IS THE MOST FAGGY GODDAMNED THING YOU COULD EVER IMAGINE, WITH THAT SAN FRANCISCO CROWD. I CAN'T SHAKE HANDS WITH ANYBODY FROM SAN FRANCISCO!

THIS MODERN WORLD--THE CARTOON THAT FEARLESSLY EXPOSES THE VENALITY OF DEAD EX-PRESIDENTS--CONSEQUENCES BE DAMNED!

TOM TOMORROW© 2000 ... tomorrow@well.com ... www.thismodernworld.com

THIS MODERN WORLD

by TOM TOMORROW

Panel 1:

IF YOU'RE A POLITICIAN, YOU CAN'T GO WRONG SUPPORTING THE *DEATH PENALTY.*

HANG 'EM *HIGH*, THAT'S WHAT *I* SAY!

CLEMENCY IS FOR *WIMPS!*

ANYBODY WANT TO HEAR MY IMPERSONATION OF A DEATH ROW INMATE PLEADING FOR HER *LIFE?*

ALPHA MALE GORE

BUSH 2000

Panel 2:

BILL CLINTON NOT ONLY *FAVORS* THIS MOST FINAL OF JUDGMENTS--HE HAS EVEN SIGNED LEGISLATION *"STREAMLINING"* THE APPEALS PROCESS.

IT'S LIKE MY MOMMA ALWAYS SAID--WHY PUT OFF A LETHAL INJECTION FOR TOMORROW WHEN YOU CAN DO IT *TODAY?*

BY THE WAY, YOU FOLKS KNOW I'M STILL *PRESIDENT*, RIGHT?

PIZZA FOR--UM--*BILL CLIFTON?* IS THERE A *BILL CLIFTON* HERE?

Panel 3:

THE PROBLEM IS THAT WE ARE *HUMAN*-- MEANING THAT OUR JUSTICE SYSTEM IS BY DEFINITION *FALLIBLE*...AFTER ALL, MORE THAN *EIGHTY PEOPLE* HAVE BEEN RELEASED FROM DEATH ROW BECAUSE THEY WERE LATER PROVEN *INNOCENT*...

WELL, YOU CAN'T MAKE AN OMELET WITHOUT BREAKING SOME *EGGS!*

YES, YOU'VE GOT TO THROW THE BABY OUT WITH THE *BATHWATER*--

--ER-- I MEAN--

OH, NEVER MIND.

Panel 4:

AND NO MATTER HOW MANY DEATH ROW CONVICTS ARE, IN FACT, GUILTY OF TERRIBLE CRIMES, ONE THING IS SIMPLY NOT DEBATABLE: IF OUR SOCIETY HAS *EVER* EXECUTED A *SINGLE INNOCENT PERSON*--

Panel 5:

--THEN WE ARE *ALL* ACCESSORIES TO *MURDER.*

Panel 6:

WELL! *THAT* ONE ENDED ON A RATHER UNPLEASANT NOTE, DIDN'T IT?

I THINK TOM TOMORROW NEEDS TO TURN HIS *FROWN* UPSIDE *DOWN!*

THIS MODERN WORLD

by TOM TOMORROW

THIS WEEK-- ANOTHER LOOK AT THE EXCITING WORLD OF

CAMPAIGN 2000!

FEATURING SPECIAL GUEST PUNDITS:

SERIOUS GUY IN A SUIT #1--

SERIOUS GUY IN A SUIT #2--

--AND-- **BLINKY** THE **VERY** NICE DOG!

ALL RIGHT, PANEL--LET'S GET STARTED! DO YOU HAVE ANY THOUGHTS ON THE END OF THE **STEVE FORBES** AND **GARY BAUER** CANDIDACIES?

WHAT A **SHOCKER!** I'M **STILL** REELING FROM THE NEWS!

YES--WHO WOULD HAVE **IMAGINED** THAT SUCH CHARISMATIC AND QUAL- IFIED MEN WOULD GAR- NER SO FEW VOTES?

MAYBE THEY'LL EACH GET TO BE PRESIDENT SOME **OTHER** TIME!

DESPITE SOME SETBACKS, GEORGE W. BUSH IS STILL FAVORED BY MANY REPUBLICANS... WHAT DO YOU THINK ACCOUNTS FOR HIS APPEAL TO THE RANK-AND-FILE?

WELL HE **IS** A "REFORMER WITH RESULTS!"

I KNOW **I'VE** ALWAYS HAD A WEAK SPOT FOR A FREQUENTLY REITERATED ALLITERATIVE PHRASE!

HIS FATHER WAS ONCE PRESIDENT, YOU KNOW!

WHAT ABOUT THE **DEMOCRATS**? ANY INSIGHT IN- TO THE RACE BETWEEN BILL BRADLEY AND AL GORE?

OH, YEAH-- I FORGOT ABOUT THOSE GUYS.

I THINK IT'S CLEAR THAT DEMO- CRATS WILL HAVE TO MAKE A CHOICE BETWEEN THE **LOUD** GUY AND THE **GRUMPY** GUY.

I'M SURE THEY ARE BOTH **VERY** NICE MEN!

FINALLY--ANY THOUGHTS ON THE "SUPER TUESDAY" PRIMARIES, WHICH MAY HAVE NARROWED THE PRES- IDENTIAL RACE DOWN TO THE TWO FINAL CANDI- DATES BY THE TIME THIS CARTOON RUNS?

IT'S ABOUT **TIME!** I DON'T THINK I COULD HAVE **TAKEN** THE SUS- PENSE MUCH **LONGER!**

YES--THE ELECTION **IS** ONLY EIGHT MONTHS AWAY, AFTER ALL!

I THINK **EVERY** TUESDAY IS A SUPER TUESDAY!

TUNE IN NEXT TIME FOR **MORE** IN-DEPTH COMMENTARY--FROM THE CARTOON THAT'S NOT AFRAID TO TACKLE THE **ISSUES!**

TOM TOMORROW © 2000 ... tomorrow@well.com ... www.thismodernworld.com

THIS MODERN WORLD

by TOM TOMORROW

I WROTE CHARLES "SPARKY" SCHULZ A FAN LETTER BACK IN '92, AND HE RESPONDED BY INVITING ME UP TO ONE SNOOPY PLACE FOR LUNCH--WHICH REALLY SAYS A LOT ABOUT THE MAN...I MEAN, I WAS JUST SOME GOOFBALL LEFT WING ALTERNATIVE PRESS GUY, AND HE WAS **CHARLES SCHULZ**, FOR CHRISSAKES--

--BUT WE WERE BOTH CARTOONISTS, AND SO HE WAS WILLING TO SPEND THE BETTER PART OF AN AFTERNOON WITH ME, DISCUSSING OUR SHARED PROFESSION...

IF I WERE A BETTER ARTIST, I'D BE A PAINTER, AND IF I WERE A BETTER WRITER, I'D WRITE BOOKS--

--BUT I'M NOT, SO I DRAW **CARTOONS!**

MORTALITY WAS ON HIS MIND EVEN THEN...HE JOKED THAT HIS ONE REGRET WAS THAT HE PROBABLY WOULD NOT BE AROUND TO VOTE AGAINST A PARTICULAR POLITICIAN IN THE '96 ELECTIONS...AND TOLD ME THAT THE STRIP WOULD DIE WITH HIM--THOUGH MAINLY BECAUSE HIS FAMILY HAD INSISTED THAT NO ONE ELSE BE ALLOWED TO TAKE IT OVER...

HOW STRANGE THAT HE PASSED AWAY AS HIS FINAL STRIP RAN IN THE WEEKEND PAPERS...THE STRIP DIDN'T DIE WITH HIM--HE DIED WITH THE STRIP.

HIS DEDICATION TO HIS CRAFT IS WORTH NOTING... A LOT OF SUCCESSFUL CARTOONISTS EMPLOY SO MANY ASSISTANTS, THEIR WORK MIGHT AS WELL BE PRODUCED ON A FACTORY LINE--BUT SCHULZ CONTINUED TO LETTER, PENCIL AND INK THE STRIP HIMSELF, EVEN AS FAILING HEALTH CAUSED HIS LINEWORK TO TREMBLE LIKE LEAVES IN A GENTLE BREEZE...

AND, ONE FINAL THOUGHT: HIS INFLUENCE ON A LOT OF US MAY NOT HAVE ALWAYS BEEN OBVIOUS, BUT IT WAS PROFOUND.

"LIFE IS FULL OF RUDE AWAKENINGS."

SIGH.

CHARLES M. SCHULZ, NOV. 26, 1922 - FEB. 12, 2000.

THIS MODERN WORLD

by TOM TOMORROW

Panel 1:

IN THE PECULIAR WEEK BEFORE SUPER TUESDAY, GEORGE BUSH RAN A SERIES OF MISLEADING ADS PAINTING JOHN McCAIN--WHOSE SISTER IS A BREAST CANCER SURVIVOR--AS AN *OPPONENT* OF BREAST CANCER RESEARCH.

I, ON THE OTHER HAND, WILL REMAIN *VERY CONCERNED* ABOUT THIS SCOURGE--

--FOR AT *LEAST* AS LONG AS IT TAKES TO DAMAGE MY OPPONENT'S CREDIBILITY!

(WATCH TO SEE HOW LONG THAT PINK RIBBON STAYS IN PLACE AFTER MARCH 7.)

Panel 2:

IN ANOTHER COMMERCIAL, FUNDED BY ONE OF BUSH'S WEALTHY SUPPORTERS, VOTERS WERE INFORMED--TO THE SURPRISE OF MANY--THAT UNLIKE THE VERY BAD JOHN McCAIN, GOV. BUSH IS ACTUALLY A *CHAMPION* OF THE ENVIRONMENT.

BUT--TEXAS HAS A *TERRIBLE* ENVIRONMENTAL RECORD! HOUSTON HAS MORE SMOG THAN *L.A!*

OH, PIFFLE! GEORGE W. BUSH IS AN ENVIRONMENTALIST WITH *EXACTITUDE!* AN ANTI-POLLUTER WITH *ANIMUS!* AN EMISSIONS CONTROLLER WITH *EMPATHY!* AN--

PLEASE BE QUIET NOW.

Panel 3:

WHICH BRINGS US, IN A ROUNDABOUT WAY, TO THE PERENNIAL QUESTION OF THIS CAMPAIGN SEASON: WHY DO REPUBLICANS TAKE THIS OPPORTUNISTIC LIGHTWEIGHT *SERIOUSLY?*

HIS YEARS AS A BUSINESSMAN GAVE HIM PLENTY OF *EXPERIENCE!*

--AT, UM, BEING BAILED OUT BY HIS FATHER'S FRIENDS.

HE'S LED ONE OF THE LARGEST STATES IN THE *NATION!*

--A STATE WHOSE CONSTITUTION GIVES THE GOVERNOR ALMOST NO ACTUAL AUTHORITY.

NEVER MIND ALL THAT! THE IMPORTANT THING IS, HE'S *ELECTABLE!*

--UNLESS, UM, HE LOSES.

Panel 4:

AFTER ALL, EVEN HIS MOST ARDENT SUPPORTERS MUST REALIZE THAT, WHILE HE MAY HAVE HIS FATHER'S *LOOKS*, HE SEEMS TO HAVE INHERITED THE *BRAINS* OF *DAN QUAYLE...*

"I'VE GOT A RECORD, A RECORD THAT IS CONSERVATIVE AND COMPASSIONATED!"

"THE SENATOR HAS GOT TO UNDERSTAND...HE CAN'T TAKE THE HIGH HORSE AND THEN CLAIM THE LOW ROAD!"

"THERE IS MADMEN IN THE WORLD, AND THERE ARE TERROR!"

"WE MUST ALL HEAR THE UNIVERSAL CALL TO LIKE YOUR NEIGHBOR JUST LIKE YOU LIKE TO BE LIKED YOURSELF!"*

* ALL GENUINE BUSH QUOTES! ARE WE HAVING *FUN* YET?

TOM TOMORROW © 3/15/00... NEW AND IMPROVED WEBSITE: www.thismodernworld.com

THIS MODERN WORLD

by TOM TOMORROW

FOR MONTHS, SCIENTISTS IN SECRET D.N.C. LABORATORIES HAVE BEEN TRYING TO PERFECT THEIR LATEST CREATION--THE *GOREBOT 2000!*

HE NEEDS TO CONVEY MORE *PASSION* AND *CONVICTION!*

NO PROBLEM--I'LL INCREASE HIS *AMPLIFICATION PARAMETERS!*

NOW WITH THE PRIMARY SEASON ALL BUT OVER, THEY BEGIN TO PREPARE FOR THE GENERAL ELECTION.

I KNOW! LET'S POSITION HIM AS A *CAMPAIGN FINANCE REFORMER!*

IT'S SO CRAZY IT JUST MIGHT *WORK!*

I'LL INPUT THE APPROPRIATE PLATITUDES *IMMEDIATELY!*

SOON, THE REPROGRAMMED GOREBOT HITS THE CAMPAIGN TRAIL WITH HIS UPGRADED MESSAGE OF *REFORM!*

SIR, YOUR FUNDRAISING EXCESSES ARE *LEGENDARY!* HOW CAN YOU *POSSIBLY* EXPECT ANYONE TO TAKE YOU SERIOUSLY ON THIS ISSUE?

I HAVE LEARNED FROM MY MISTAKES!

NEXT QUESTION PLEASE!

PRESS

GOREBOT 2000

CLICK! WHIRRRR!

WILL THE VOTERS *BUY* IT? STAY *TUNED!*

HE'S REALLY *CHANGED!* HE SEEMS MORE *PASSIONATE* SOMEHOW!

I THINK WE SHOULD JUDGE HIM BY HIS *WORDS*, RATHER THAN HIS *DEEDS!*

YES--IF HE *SAYS* HE IS OPPOSED TO SOFT MONEY, IT *MUST* BE TRUE!

THIS MODERN WORLD

by TOM TOMORROW

ACCORDING TO THE EXPERTS, THE AMERICAN ECONOMY HAS ACHIEVED *FULL EMPLOYMENT*—MEANING, AS WE RECENTLY HEARD A NETWORK NEWS CORRESPONDENT ENTHUSIASTICALLY EXPLAIN, THAT THESE DAYS—

—THERE'S A JOB FOR *EVERYONE WHO WANTS ONE!*

Nightly News

YES, PROSPERITY ABOUNDS...AND WE'RE SURE ALL THOSE FULLY EMPLOYED PEOPLE OUT THERE FLIPPING BURGERS AND EMPTYING TRASH CANS ARE JUST AS EXCITED ABOUT IT AS *WE* ARE!

HOW FORTUNATE WE ARE TO SHARE IN OUR NATION'S ECONOMIC ABUNDANCE.

IF I AM LUCKY, I MAY HAVE ENOUGH MONEY LEFT OVER AT THE END OF THE MONTH TO GO SEE A *MOVIE!*

I MIGHT EVEN BE ABLE TO AFFORD *POPCORN!*

WACKY BURGER
ONLY 99

Sugar Water

OF COURSE, THIS UNBRIDLED GOOD FORTUNE *DOES* MAKE *ALAN GREENSPAN* A BIT NERVOUS...

MILLIONS OF PREVIOUSLY UNEMPLOYED AMERICANS NOW HAVE LOUSY JOBS MAKING BARELY ENOUGH TO SURVIVE?

THIS IS *TERRIBLE!* I'VE GOT TO RAISE INTEREST RATES *IMMEDIATELY!*

The Daily Record
GOOD TIMES HERE
Burger King is Hiring!
Taco Bell Also Has Openings

BUT WE SHOULDN'T BE TOO *HARD* ON THE MAN... AFTER ALL, HE JUST WANTS TO KEEP UNEMPLOYMENT AT A NICE, SAFE LEVEL—SO THE PARTY CAN GO ON FOR THE *REST* OF US!

COMING UP NEXT—WE GO LIVE TO THE 79TH STREET BOAT BASIN FOR UNDENIABLE PROOF THAT A RISING TIDE LIFTS *ALL BOATS!*

EXCEPT UM, FOR THE ONES THAT SINK.

FIRST, THESE MESSAGES!

Nightly News

THIS MODERN WORLD

by TOM TOMORROW

IMAGINE THAT YOU'RE STANDING ON A NEW YORK CITY STREET CORNER, MINDING YOUR OWN BUSINESS, TRYING TO HAIL A CAB.

> I HOPE REGIS PHILBIN IS ABLE TO SETTLE HIS SALARY DISPUTE WITH ABC.

> I WONDER IF PIGEONS ARE SMARTER THAN RATS.

> HUMM DE DUM DE DUM...LIVIN' LA VIDA LOCA...

A MENACING THUG APPROACHES YOU AND ASKS IF YOU HAVE ANY ILLEGAL DRUGS FOR SALE...YOU RESPOND ANGRILY...

> YO, MAN, GOT ANY WEED?

> WHAT--? GET *AWAY* FROM ME, YOU LOW-LIFE!

A SCUFFLE ENSUES...MORE THUGS APPEAR OUT OF NOWHERE AND SURROUND YOU...THEY'RE SHOUTING SOMETHING BUT EVERYTHING IS MOVING MUCH TOO QUICKLY AND ONE OF THEM PULLS OUT A GUN...

> ...AND SUDDENLY YOU'RE BLEEDING TO DEATH IN THE STREET.

> I *SAID* I WAS A PO-LICE OFFICER!

> IS THERE *NO* RESPECT FOR THE LAW ANYMORE?

> URK

FORTUNATELY, NOTHING LIKE THAT COULD EVER *REALLY* HAPPEN... *RIGHT*?

> *CERTAINLY NOT!*--AT LEAST, NOT AS LONG AS YOU'RE A WELL-DRESSED *WHITE PERSON!*

> IT'S OPEN SEASON ON THE *REST* OF YOU, OF COURSE.

> GOTTA KEEP THE STREETS *SAFE*, YOU KNOW!

THIS MODERN WORLD

by TOM TOMORROW

HEY, EVERYONE! IT'S TIME ONCE AGAIN FOR...

DR. DEBBIE'S RADIO ADVICE SHOW!!

SHE KNOWS WHAT'S *BEST* FOR YOU!

"NOW GO DO WHAT I *SAY*™!"

HELLO, CALLER--THIS IS DR. DEBBIE! WHAT CAN I HELP YOU WITH TODAY?

HELLO, DR. DEBBIE! I'VE GOT A PROB-LEM WITH MY *HUSBAND*--

YOUR *HUS-BAND*? HA! I SAY *DUMP* THE JERK! GET *ON* WITH YOUR LIFE!

BUT--I--YOU SEE--

WHAT PART OF "DUMP THE JERK" DON'T YOU *UNDERSTAND*? JEEZ--YOU *PEOPLE*! OKAY, NEXT CALL!

THANKS FOR TAKING MY CALL, DR. DEBBIE! I'VE GOT A SITUATION WITH MY *GRANDMOTHER*--

OH, YOU'VE GOT A "SITUATION" DO YOU? WELL FOR CRYIN' OUT LOUD-- DO YOU THINK YOU'RE THE ONLY PERSON IN THE WORLD WITH *PROBLEMS*? WELL? *DO* YOU? *ANSWER* ME!

WELL--NO--BUT--

NO "BUTS" ABOUT IT, LADY! THE WORLD DOESN'T REVOLVE AROUND YOU--AND IT'S ABOUT TIME YOU *REALIZED* IT! OKAY! LET'S SEE WHO WE'VE GOT ON LINE *THREE*!

UM--DR. DEBBIE? I WAS JUST *WONDER-ING*--

YOU WERE *WONDERING*, WERE YOU? WELL WHY NOT STOP *WON-DERING* AND START *DOING* SOMETHING? HOW DO YOU EVER EXPECT TO MAKE ANYTHING OF YOURSELF IF YOU SIT AROUND *WONDERING* ALL DAY?

NOW GET OFF YOUR DUFF AND *"GO DO WHAT I SAY*™!" WE'LL BE BACK AFTER THESE MESSAGES!

NEED SOME ADVICE FROM A TOTAL STRANGER ON THE RADIO? CALL 1-800-*DEBBIE*!

TOM TOMORROW© 5-3-00 ... tomorrow@well.com ... www.thismodernworld.com

THIS MODERN WORLD

by TOM TOMORROW

A LOT OF AMERICANS ARE PRETTY DARNED SUS-PICIOUS ABOUT THIS WHOLE CENSUS THING--AND IT'S NO WONDER!

HAH! THEY WANT TO KNOW HOW MUCH MONEY I MAKE! ANYONE WHO WOULD WILLINGLY HAND OVER THAT KIND OF PERSONAL INFORMATION TO THE GOVERNMENT WOULD HAVE TO BE SOME KIND OF--

--TAXPAYER?

OH, WHO ASKED YOU?

CITIZENS WHO RECEIVED THE LONG FORM HAVE PARTICULAR CAUSE FOR CONCERN!

OH SURE, THEY SAY THEY WANT TO KNOW WHEN WE GO TO WORK SO THEY CAN BETTER MANAGE THE FLOW OF RUSH HOUR TRAFFIC--

--BUT WHAT IF THEY JUST WANT TO KNOW WHEN THEY CAN BREAK INTO OUR HOUSES AND ROB US BLIND?

DIDJA EVER THINK OF THAT?

WHY--WHO KNOWS HOW THE INFORMATION THEY WANT COULD BE USED AGAINST US?

YEAH--WHY WOULD THEY CARE IF WE LIVE IN A MOBILE HOME OR NOT--

--UNLESS THEY WANT TO KNOW WHERE THEIR SECRET WEATHER CON-TROL MACHINES SHOULD SEND THE TORNADOES?

SO FOR GOD'S SAKE, PEOPLE--THROW THOSE CEN-SUS FORMS AWAY--BEFORE IT'S TOO LATE!

TOM TOMORROW SAYS HE RENTS AN APART-MENT WITH COMPLETE PLUMBING FACILITIES--AND HAS A TELEPHONE CAPABLE OF MAKING AND RECEIVING CALLS!*

AND THE FOOL GAVE US THIS INFORMATION VOLUNTARILY? WELL, HE'LL CERTAINLY RE-GRET THAT SOON ENOUGH!

BWAH HA HA HA!

CENSUS BUREAU
DIVISION OF GLOBAL DOMINATION

*ACTUAL LONG FORM QUESTIONS.

TOM TOMORROW© 4-5-00 ... tomorrow@well.com ... www.thismodernworld.com

THIS MODERN WORLD

by TOM TOMORROW

NOTE: The satirical commentary which follows will undoubtedly provide most readers with more cartoon satisfaction than they ever dreamed possible. However, a recalcitrant minority may find this week's offering predictable, heavy-handed, or otherwise disagreeable. Fortunately, there's something for them as well:

A RAINY DAY FUN GAME!

That's right! You see, we've *deliberately inserted* numerous mistakes throughout the following four panels. Can you spot them all? We believe the attempt to do so will provide untold hours of non-partisan entertainment!

1. SO, LET'S SEE, BIFF-- IN D.C., PROTESTERS WERE SUBJECTED TO TEAR GAS, UNJUSTIFIED ARREST SWEEPS, THE CLOSURE OF THEIR HEADQUARTERS ON THE FLIMSIEST OF PRETEXTS--

--ISN'T THIS THE SORT OF SUPPRESSION OF DISSENT WE ALWAYS ACCUSE OUR *ENEMIES* OF PRACTICING?

2. OH, GET OVER IT, SPARKY! THOSE PROTESTERS WERE JUST A BUNCH OF UNION *THUGS* AND LONG-HAIRED *WEIRDOS* TRYING TO RE-LIVE THE *SIXTIES!*

THEY NEED TO CALL AMTRAK AND RESERVE SOME SEATS ON THE *CLUE TRAIN*, MY FRIEND!

3. GLOBALIZATION IS A FACT OF LIFE AND THERE'S NOTHING YOUR TREE-HUGGING, BLEEDING HEART COMRADES CAN *DO* ABOUT IT! THEY NEED TO STOP WHINING ABOUT "HUMAN RIGHTS" AND "ENVIRONMENTAL CONCERNS" AND *GET WITH THE PROGRAM!*

4. SO INSTEAD OF *PROTESTING* THE ECONOMIC RAPE OF THE WORLD-- --THEY SHOULD JUST *LIE BACK* AND *ENJOY* IT!

DID YOU *SPOT THE MISTAKES?*

1. When Sparky says "we," he is clearly referring to government officials and their apologists, of which he is neither. Whoops!

2. Amtrak doesn't really operate a "clue train."

3. An actual defender of the I.M.F. would be unlikely to phrase his arguments in quite this manner.

4. Sparky is talking about the protesters-- but Biff's rejoinder seems to refer to the third world nations affected by I.M.F. structural adjustment policies. Whoops again!

SPECIAL NOTE TO READERS PLANNING TO LET US KNOW THAT OUR ENTIRE POINT OF VIEW IS A MISTAKE: Ha, ha! Good one! We sure didn't see that coming!

TOM TOMORROW© 4-29-00 ... tomorrow@well.com ... www.thismodernworld.com

113

THIS MODERN WORLD

by TOM TOMORROW

SURE, THE REVIEWS HAVE BEEN LOUSY! THAT'S BECAUSE THE LIBERAL MEDIA DON'T **WANT** YOU TO SEE ONE OF THE MOST IMPORTANT MOVIES OF OUR AGE--

BATTLEFIELD WASHINGTON

A SAGA OF THE YEAR 2000*

*BASED ON THE WORK OF **L. RONALD REAGAN**, FOUNDER OF THE CHURCH OF **REPUBLICANOLOGY**!

YOU'LL **GASP** AT THE SHOCKING ARROGANCE OF THE EVIL **DEMOCRAT OVERLORD** AND HIS SCHEMING **SECOND-IN-COMMAND**!

PATHETIC REPUBLICANS! I SHOULD **CRUSH** THEM LIKE THE INSECTS THEY **ARE**!

THE FOOL! SOON HIS POWER WILL BE **MINE**!

YOU'LL **CHEER** AS A DASHING YOUNG REBEL VENTURES FORTH FROM HIS SIMPLE HOMELAND AND BECOMES A **LEADER** IN THE STRUGGLE AGAINST **TYRANNY**!

WE MUST NOT **FIGHT**, JOHN McCAIN! WE MUST JOIN FORCES TO DEFEAT THE **DEVILS-WHO-RULE**!

YEAH, YEAH, ALL RIGHT...WHATEVER...

AND YOU'LL BE ON THE **EDGE OF YOUR SEAT** AS THE FINAL CONFRONTATION NEARS ITS **CLIMAX**--WITH THE FATE OF A **NATION** HANGING IN THE BALANCE!

VOTE FOR **GORE**, STUPID MAN-ANIMALS--OR BE **DESTROYED**!

NO! RISE UP--FOR SCHOOL VOUCHERS! AND FAITH-BASED INITIATIVES!

AND SOME OTHER STUFF MY ADVISORS TOLD ME TO SAY!

REPUBLICANOLOGY WILL SET YOU **FREE**!

DEBATE 2000

TOM TOMORROW© 5-25-00 ... tomorrow@well.com ... www.thismodernworld.com

THIS MODERN WORLD

by TOM TOMORROW

THE SUCCESS OF FILMMAKERS LIKE THE *FARRELLY BROTHERS* AND THOSE *SOUTH PARK* GUYS MAKES IT PRETTY CLEAR, SPARKY--WHAT THE KIDS TO-DAY WANT IS *LOWBROW GROSS-OUT HUMOR!*

IF WE WANT TO INCREASE AUDIENCE SHARE, WE'VE *GOT* TO JETTISON THE LONG-WINDED POLITICAL STUFF--AND FOCUS INSTEAD ON *BODILY FLUIDS!*

HMMM...

I *WAS* GOING TO DISCUSS THE SHORT-SIGHTED LUNACY OF INVESTING SOCIAL SECUR-ITY FUNDS IN THE *STOCK MARKET* THIS WEEK--BUT MAYBE YOU'RE *RIGHT!* MAY-BE WE NEED TO BE A LITTLE MORE--WELL--

--CUTTING EDGE!!

WHUMP!

NOW *THAT'S* A FUNNY CARTOON! COMEDY CEN-TRAL, HERE WE COME!

DON'T WORRY, KIDS! HE'LL BE BACK NEXT WEEK--JUST LIKE *KENNY!*

TOM TOMORROW © 1999

THIS MODERN WORLD

by TOM TOMORROW

SO AS SUPERPOWER CONFRONTATIONS GO, THE RECENT GAME OF BRINKSMANSHIP BETWEEN *TIME WARNER* AND *ABC-DISNEY* WASN'T EXACTLY UP THERE WITH THE *CUBAN MISSILE CRISIS*...

THOUGH WE *WERE* DENIED ACCESS TO SEVERAL OF OUR *FAVORITE PRO-GRAMS*!

AT LEAST, UNTIL WE HOOKED UP THE AN-TENNA.

BUT THE SIGNAL WAS STILL *SOMEWHAT INDISTINCT*!

...BUT IT DID GIVE US AN INDICATION OF HOW THE "CLINTON ADMINISTRATION POLICY OF PROMOTING *CONSOLIDATION*...AS A WAY OF ENCOURAGING *COMPETITION*" (TO QUOTE THOSE MASTERS OF ORWELLIAN PROSE AT THE *NEW YORK TIMES*) IS LIKELY TO BENEFIT *CONSUMERS*...

FREEDOM IS *SLAVERY*!

IGNORANCE IS *STRENGTH*!

MONOPOLIES OFFER *CHOICE*!

BIG BUSINESS IS WATCHING YOU!

...WHICH IS TO SAY, IN MUCH THE SAME WAY THAT THE "COMPETITION" BETWEEN GIANT RADIOAC-TIVE MONSTERS BENEFITTED *TOKYO* IN THOSE OLD *GODZILLA* MOVIES...

RRRRARGH!

WE HAVE SO MANY *OPTIONS*!

I DON'T KNOW WHETHER I'D RATHER BE *TRAMPLED* --OR *ROASTED ALIVE*!

...OR--PERHAPS MORE APPROPRIATELY-- IN THE WAY THAT THE "COMPETITION" BETWEEN TWO BOUGHT-AND-PAID-FOR *PRESIDENTIAL CANDIDATES* IS LIKELY TO BENEFIT *DEMOCRACY*...

--WHICH IS WHY I AM TAKING THIS OPPORTUNITY TO ANNOUNCE *MY* CAN-DIDACY FOR PRESIDENT OF THE UNITED STATES--

--BECAUSE *YOU COULD DO A LOT WORSE THIS YEAR!**

?

DOES NOT COMPUTE

*PAID FOR BY THE COMMITTEE THAT WOULD RATHER VOTE FOR A DAMNED PENGUIN THAN THOSE OTHER TWO LOSERS.

TOM TOMORROW © 5-17-00 ... tomorrow@well.com ... www.thismodernworld.com

116

HELLO, EVERYONE-- AND WELCOME TO **HOLOGRAPHIC DICK CLARK'S NEW YEAR'S ROCKIN' EVE: 2999!**

I'M THE HOLOGRAPHIC SIMULATION OF THE HUMAN KNOWN AS *DICK CLARK*, AND I'M HERE WITH *OVERLORD SPLARKTOW*, SUPREME COMMANDER OF THE NORTHEASTERN QUADRANT!

GREETINGS, DICK! IT APPEARS THAT THE EARTHLINGS HAVE BEEN CORRALLED INTO THEIR DESIGNATED CELEBRATION SECTORS MOST EFFICIENTLY!

ER, YES, IT *IS* QUITE A CROWD OUT THERE! AND SINCE WE'VE STILL GOT A FEW MINUTES BEFORE THE BALL DROPS, I AM PROGRAMMED TO FILL THE TIME WITH A LOOK BACK AT THE MILLENNIUM--AND WHAT A WACKY THOUSAND YEARS IT'S BEEN!

AND REMEMBER, HUMANS--YOU ARE NOT AUTHORIZED TO ACCESS MOOD-ALTERING SUBSTANCES UNTIL 23:59!

AS WE ALL KNOW, THE MILLENNIUM BEGAN WITH THE FAMOUS "Y2K GLITCH"--WHICH CREATED *UNPRECEDENTED HARDSHIPS* FOR THE CITIZENS OF THE ERA!

I HAD TO WAIT *SEVERAL HOURS* TO GET NEW CABLE SERVICE INSTALLED!

I WAS ON HOLD WITH BELL ATLANTIC FOR *FORTY-FIVE MINUTES!*

WILL LIFE *EVER* GET BACK TO NORMAL?

MORE SIGNIFICANTLY, A POLITICAL MILESTONE WAS REACHED LATER THAT CENTURY WHEN *DONALD TRUMP'S* CRYOGENICALLY PRESERVED *BRAIN* WAS ELECTED *PRESIDENT* OF THE NORTH AMERICAN FEDERATION!

I MAY JUST BE A BRAIN IN A VAT OF CHEMICALS--BUT I *STILL* DATE THE WORLD'S MOST BEAUTIFUL WOMEN!

AND I'M *PRESIDENT!*

EAT YOUR HEARTS OUT, SUCKERS!

TIME FOR YOUR *NUTRIENT BATH*, STUDMUFFIN!

BY THE 23RD CENTURY, OF COURSE, THE OLD NATION-STATES WERE BECOMING AN ANACHRONISM...THE TURNING POINT CAME WHEN SEVERAL MULTI-NATIONAL CORPORATIONS WERE GIVEN SEATS ON THE U.N. SECURITY COUNCIL...

IF COCA-COLA REFUSES TO SIGN THE NUCLEAR TEST BAN TREATY--ALL OF OUR EFFORTS WILL HAVE BEEN WASTED!

RELAX, AMBASSADOR! HERE-- HAVE A COKE AND A SMILE!

MICROSOFT

COCA-COLA

IN FACT, MOST POLITICAL OFFICES WERE PURELY CEREMONIAL BY THEN... ELECTIONS WERE HELD SOLELY FOR THE ENTERTAINMENT THEY PROVIDED-- AND WITH HOLOGRAPHIC IMAGING NOW COMMON-PLACE, YOU NEVER KNEW WHO MIGHT TOSS A HAT IN THE RING...

VLAD THE IMPALER'S A LITTLE HARSH ON SOCIAL ISSUES--BUT I REALLY LIKE HIS PLAN TO REDUCE THE DEFICIT!

WELL, CELINE DION PROMISES TO BRING US TOGETHER THROUGH THE MAGIC OF SONG!

VOTE FOR VLAD

IN 2678, THE GLOBAL POPULATION REACHED 600 BILLION... ENVIRONMENTALISTS WONDERED IF THE PLANET COULD SUSTAIN SUCH GROWTH, BUT A POPULAR CYBERNET HOST SCOFFED AT THEIR CONCERNS...

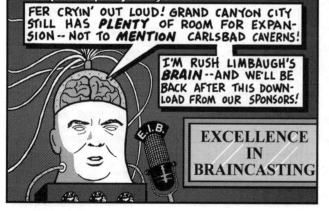

FER CRYIN' OUT LOUD! GRAND CANYON CITY STILL HAS PLENTY OF ROOM FOR EXPANSION -- NOT TO MENTION CARLSBAD CAVERNS!

I'M RUSH LIMBAUGH'S BRAIN --AND WE'LL BE BACK AFTER THIS DOWN-LOAD FROM OUR SPONSORS!

E.I.B.

EXCELLENCE
IN
BRAINCASTING

NONETHELESS, BIOLOGICAL REPRODUCTION SOON BE-CAME SOCIALLY SUSPECT... BY THE 2700s, UN-REPENTANT HETEROSEXUAL "BREEDERS" WERE AN OPPRESSED, IF OUTSPOKEN, MINORITY...

WE'RE STRAIGHT-- WE MATE-- GET USED TO IT!!

PERVERTS.

MOST HISTORIANS AGREE THAT THE GOLDEN AGE OF MANKIND BEGAN IN THE 29TH CENTURY, WHEN POPULATION GROWTH WAS STABILIZED THROUGH THE **OFFICIAL CLONING ACT**...NOW, NOT ONLY DID EVERYONE WEAR THE SAME BRANDS AND EAT AT THE SAME FRANCHISES--BUT THEY ALL **LOOKED** EXACTLY THE SAME AS WELL!

LIFE IS MUCH SIMPLER THIS WAY--DON'T YOU AGREE, DAVID 40928423?

ABSOLUTELY, DAVID 320329!

DURING THIS NEW DAWN OF ENLIGHTENMENT, SOCIETY REORDERED ITS **PRIORITIES**... ACTORS AND MUSICIANS CAME TO BE VIEWED AS CONTEMPTIBLE **BORES**--WHERAS **CARTOONISTS** WERE NOW TREATED AS **GODS!**

THEIR TRENCHANT INTERTWINING OF HUMOR AND COMMENTARY IS SURELY HUMANITY'S CROWNING ACHIEVEMENT!

YES--WITHOUT CARTOONS, WE ARE LITTLE BETTER THAN **ANIMALS!**

AND SO, IN THE YEAR 2999, HUMANITY'S DREAM OF FLYING CARS, DOMED CITIES, VIDEOPHONES, AND FOOD PILLS WAS AT LAST REALIZED...WAR, POVERTY, DISEASE, AND INJUSTICE WERE ELIMINATED, AND CITIZENS LOOKED FORWARD TO A NEW MILLENNIUM OF PEACE AND PROSPERITY...

AND CARTOONS, OF COURSE.

WELL, THAT GOES WITHOUT SAYING.

...AND THEN THE OVERLORDS FROM PLANET ZOLTRON ARRIVED, SLAUGHTERING MOST OF THE POPULATION AND ENSLAVING THE REST.

BOY, TALK ABOUT A Y3K GLITCH! HA, HA! HAPPY NEW YEAR, OVERLORD SPLARKTOW!

HAPPY NEW YEAR, DICK. A BRIEF PERIOD OF CELEBRATION MAY NOW COMMENCE.

SLAVE-LABOR CAMPS WILL RESUME OPERATION AT 0600 HOURS. END TRANSMISSION.

(ORIGINALLY APPEARED IN *THE NEW YORKER*.)

119

ABOUT THE AUTHOR

TOM TOMORROW'S cartoons run in newspapers all over the damn place and have appeared in magazines from *The Nation* to *The New Yorker* to *TV Guide*. (Yes, that's right—*TV Guide*.) He's the recipient of various honors, including the Robert F. Kennedy Journalism Award, and has recently been added to the rotating roster on the Spitfire spoken word tour, at the suggestion of rantmaster extraordinaire Jello Biafra, to whom he is much indebted. He lives in Brooklyn, New York, with his wife and several cats, and frankly finds it somewhat uncomfortable to speak of himself in the third person, which is why he has put off writing this paragraph for months and months until it has come to the point that his editor is likely to take the F train to his neighborhood in Brooklyn and do him bodily harm if he does not turn something in this very afternoon. The problem is, he is never quite certain what to write about himself for these things, because really, when you think about it, the standard paragraph reciting publications and awards and residency and all that sort of thing is kind of a cop-out, which, though it appears under the heading "About the Author," actually tells you very little about the author at all. Of course, the author in this particular case doesn't know how much information about himself he really wants to share with you anyway, though he can see how certain biographical details might add to a deeper understanding of his work. For instance, he has lived in ten different states in his lifetime, including several throughout the South, a fact which is relevant to his commentary on the Confederate flag controversy, belying the assumption of many readers that he is a "know nothing piss-pot Yankee," as one fellow put it, or more generally, some kind of East Coast elitist snob who wouldn't know a real American if one were to come up to him on the street and bite him on the nose. On the other hand, the author in this case is a cartoonist, and cartoonists are always expected to maintain the public illusion that they are wacky, wacky people who don't take anything seriously—even if they are in reality moody people who take many things far too seriously—so there is a temptation for the author/cartoonist to be flippant and devil-may-care, and to perhaps write a paragraph about himself containing many obvious fictions, to say that he is ninety-eight years old and a former astronaut, and that Beanie Babies are his true passion in life, ha ha—but that's been done so many times that it has become a formula unto itself, and the author is uncomfortable with that as well.

Ultimately, the author would like you to know that he is probably far less interesting than you might imagine, given that most of his time is spent sitting around alone in a small cluttered room thinking about stuff. But he sure loves those Beanie Babies. Ha, ha.